"I marvel at Michael Hagemeister's capacity to shed light on the darkest, the most consequential of all conspiratorial works of the modern age. He knows so well how to make sense of the resonance of nonsense, its persuasiveness and troubling persistence."

Steven J. Zipperstein, *Daniel E. Koshland Professor in Jewish Culture and History at Stanford University, USA, and author of* Pogrom: Kishinev and the Tilt of History

"This collection of studies by the intellectual historian Michael Hagemeister sheds penetrating light on the many puzzles and myths surrounding *The Protocols of the Elders of Zion*, which since its first publication in Russia in 1903 has become a staple of antisemitic and conspirological discourse worldwide. Each of his articles, based on extensive archival research and displaying an enviable mastery of the vast polemical and scholarly literature devoted to the notorious forgery, deals with a different aspect of the *Protocols*: these range from when and by whom they were produced, what happened at the famous Bern trial in the 1930s, to the place of the document in apocalyptic speculations in today's Russia. In particular, Hagemeister shows that the theory favored by Norman Cohn and many others, according to which the *Protocols* were created by the Tsarist secret police, is deeply flawed, and the biography of Sergei Nilus, a key early editor and publisher of the *Protocols*, has been vastly distorted in recent fictional and other treatments. Hagemeister's book is a significant contribution and will be of great interest to scholars in many fields."

Henryk Baran, *Professor of Slavic Literature at the University at Albany, SUNY, USA*

"Michael Hagemeister is certainly the best specialist on the Russian and German history of *The Protocols of the Elders of Zion*, the most famous forgery in Western history. But, as the studies gathered in this book show, he has also explored the field of the international circulation of the forgery and analysed its various political uses. This historian and philologist, author of a large number of works of exceptional rigour and erudition, has done pioneering work in showing that, concerning the origins and worldwide dissemination of the *Protocols*, the elementary norms of historical research had been ignored in favour of a multitude of fictional accounts, constructed from 1921 onwards on the basis of the recollections of various supposed witnesses, many of whom were false witnesses. Through his unparalleled research on the best- and long-selling conspiracy and apocalyptic literature, based on a demystifying critique of carefully contextualised texts and documents, Michael Hagemeister has brilliantly contributed to a scientific history of modern political myths and utopias."

Pierre-André Taguieff, *philosopher and historian of ideas,*
Director of Research at the CNRS, France, and author of
Les Protocoles des Sages de Sion: Faux et usages d'un faux

The Perennial Conspiracy Theory

The Perennial Conspiracy Theory is a collection of essays on *The Protocols of the Elders of Zion*, a fake document which has created a pernicious antisemitic conspiracy theory.

The author analyses the murky origins of this notorious forgery and the contested claims of authorship. He explores the impact of the *Protocols* on various countries during the interwar years including Soviet Russia, the United Kingdom, France, Nazi Germany, and the United States. He also profiles figures closely associated with the dissemination of antisemitic conspiracy theories, such as Sergei Nilus and Leslie Fry, as well as examining the controversies arising from the famous Bern trial related to the *Protocols*. The book concludes with an assessment of the ongoing influence of the *Protocols* in post-Soviet Russia.

This volume will be of interest to researchers and students working in the fields of antisemitism, conspiracy theories, the far right, Jewish studies, and modern history.

Michael Hagemeister has lectured in Russian (Intellectual) History at universities in Germany, Austria, and Switzerland.

Routledge Studies in Fascism and the Far Right
Series editors
Nigel Copsey, Teesside University, UK and Graham Macklin, Center for Research on Extremism (C-REX), University of Oslo, Norway

This book series focuses upon national, transnational and global manifestations of fascist, far right and right-wing politics primarily within a historical context but also drawing on insights and approaches from other disciplinary perspectives. Its scope also includes anti-fascism, radical-right populism, extreme-right violence and terrorism, cultural manifestations of the far right, and points of convergence and exchange with the mainstream and traditional right.

Titles include:

Imagining Far-right Terrorism
Violence, Immigration, and the Nation State in Contemporary Western Europe
Josefin Graef

Male Supremacism in the United States
From Patriarchal Traditionalism to Misogynist Incels and the Alt-Right
Edited by Emily K. Carian, Alex DiBranco and Chelsea Ebin

The Fascist Faith Of Romania's Legion "Archangel Michael" in Romania, 1927–41
Martyrdom To National Purification
Constantin Iordachi

A Transnational History of Right-Wing Terrorism
Political Violence and the Far Right in Eastern and Western Europe since 1900
Edited by Johannes Dafinger and Moritz Florin

For more information about this series, please visit: www.routledge.com/Routledge-Studies-in-Fascism-and-the-Far-Right/book-series/FFR

The Perennial Conspiracy Theory

Reflections on the History of
The Protocols of the Elders of Zion

Michael Hagemeister

R Routledge
Taylor & Francis Group

LONDON AND NEW YORK

First published 2022
by Routledge
2 Park Square, Milton Park, Abingdon, Oxon OX14 4RN

and by Routledge
605 Third Avenue, New York, NY 10158

Routledge is an imprint of the Taylor & Francis Group, an informa business

© 2022 Michael Hagemeister

The right of Michael Hagemeister to be identified as author of this work has been asserted in accordance with sections 77 and 78 of the Copyright, Designs and Patents Act 1988.

Figure 5.1: From THE PLOT: THE SECRET STORY OF THE PROTOCOLS OF THE ELDERS OF ZION by Will Eisner. Copyright © 2005 by Will Eisner Studios, Inc. Used by permission of W. W. Norton and Company, Inc.

Every effort has been made to contact copyright-holders. Please advise the publisher of any errors or omissions, and these will be corrected in subsequent editions.

British Library Cataloguing-in-Publication Data
A catalogue record for this book is available from the British Library

Library of Congress Cataloging-in-Publication Data
A catalog record has been requested for this book

ISBN: 978-1-032-06015-6 (hbk)
ISBN: 978-1-032-06116-0 (pbk)
ISBN: 978-1-003-20078-9 (ebk)

DOI: 10.4324/9781003200789

Typeset in Times New Roman
by Deanta Global Publishing Services, Chennai, India

In memory of Richard S. Levy
(1940–2021)

Contents

Figures

Preface

In the summer of 1903, a series of articles with the title "Programme for World Conquest by the Jews" was published in an obscure right-wing newspaper in Saint Petersburg. The newspaper itself folded soon after; only a few rare copies can now be found in select libraries. However, the text itself, which appeared in print here for the first time, was to have an extraordinary career. Largely ignored at the time, it had, by the 1920s, been translated into all major world languages.

The text came to be known as *The Protocols of the Elders of Zion*, an anonymous work of uncertain genre (dubbed 'protocols' only by subsequent editors). It is generally known that this is a vicious antisemitic pamphlet describing the alleged plan of a worldwide Jewish conspiracy. Why, then, waste one's time reading a work said to be nothing but a blatant forgery – a most dangerous one at that, serving as it does as a "license to murder" or as a "warrant for genocide"?

In fact, this was exactly how I responded to Russian friends when they asked me in the 1980s to bring them a copy of this legend-shrouded text on one of my next visits. At that time, I often travelled to Moscow to do research for my doctoral thesis, which examined the life and thought of Nikolai Fëdorov, a nineteenth-century Russian philosopher. This research brought me into dissident circles of national conservatives, who had preserved this ideological outlook under the conditions of Soviet rule.

Until then, I too had only heard about the *Protocols* but had not read them. The wish of my Russian friends was fulfilled without it being necessary for me to do anything. At the end of the 1980s – it was the time of *perestroika* – censorship fell and copies of the *Protocols* were sold for a few rubles on almost every street corner. Even in the circle of my friends, the text was eagerly discussed and quite a few believed to find in it the explanation for the sorrowful history of their country in the twentieth century.

Now I also began to take an interest in the *Protocols* and soon realised that the information about their origin was vague and contradictory. Since access to Russian archives became much easier at the beginning of the 1990s and some archives became accessible for the first time, my hope was that I would be able to solve one or two of the mysteries surrounding the *Protocols*. Now, three decades later, during which I have worked in thirty archives in ten countries, many questions still remain open. I will leave them to future researchers. To make their work a little easier, this volume makes available some of the results of my research.

While preparing the present edition, I learned that Richard S. Levy has passed away. This book is dedicated to his memory.

Bochum, August 2021

Acknowledgments

Chapter 1 is a revised version of the article "A fake conquers the world – *The Protocols of the Elders of Zion*", in: Andrea Mork and Tessa Ryan, eds., *Fake (f)or Real. A History of Forgery and Falsification*, Luxembourg: Publications Office of the European Union, 2020, pp. 155–171.

Chapter 2 is a thoroughly revised and extended version of the article "*The Protocols of the Elders of Zion* in Court. The Bern trials, 1933–1937", in: Esther Webman, ed., *The Global Impact of* The Protocols of the Elders of Zion: *A century-old myth*. London, New York: Routledge 2011, pp. 241–253.

Chapter 3 first appeared under the title "Zur Frühgeschichte der 'Protokolle der Weisen von Zion'. Das verschollene Exemplar der Lenin-Bibliothek", in: Eva Horn and Michael Hagemeister, eds., *Die Fiktion von der jüdischen Weltverschwörung. Zu Text und Kontext der "Protokolle der Weisen von Zion"*, Göttingen: Wallstein Verlag, 2012, pp. 161–189.

Chapter 4 is a revised and updated version of the article "The American Connection. Leslie Fry and the *Protocols of the Elders of Zion*", in: Marina Ciccarini et al., eds., *Kesarevo Kesarju: Scritti in onore di Cesare G. De Michelis*, Florence: Firenze University Press, 2014, pp. 217–228. I am indebted to Reinhard Markner for his valuable comments and to Andrew McKenzie-McHarg for his help in translating this article.

Chapter 5 is a thoroughly revised, enlarged and updated version of the article "'The Antichrist as an Imminent Political Possibility': Sergei Nilus and the Apocalyptical Reading of the 'Protocols of the Elders of Zion'", in: Steven T. Katz and Richard Landes, eds., *The Paranoid Apocalypse: A Hundred-Year Retrospective on 'The Protocols of the Elders of Zion'*, New York: New York University Press, 2012, pp. 79–91.

Chapter 6 is a revised and updated version of the article "The Third Rome Against the Third Temple. Apocalypticism and Conspiracism in Post-Soviet Russia", in: Asbjørn Dyrendal et al., eds., *Handbook of Conspiracy Theory and Contemporary Religion*, Leiden: Brill, 2018, pp. 423–442.

I thank the publishers mentioned for their kind permission to reprint the articles.

For the permission to reprint the images, I thank Staatsarchiv des Kantons Bern (2.1), Archiv für Zeitgeschichte, Zurich (2.3, 2.4, 2.5, 3.2, 3.3, 3.4, 3.5), Special Collections and Archives, Oviatt Library, California State University, Northridge (4.1), W.W. Norton and Company, Inc. (5.1).

This book was initiated by Craig Fowlie and supervised by Hannah Rich. I would like to take this opportunity to thank them and all those involved in its production.

1 A fake conquers the world

The Protocols of the Elders of Zion

This chapter gives an overview of *The Protocols of the Elders of Zion*. First, the central ideas of the text are outlined, the plan of the conspiracy, the strategy, tactics, and objectives. Then the question of literary genre is discussed: Is it a negative utopia, a programme for world conquest, or the "Charter of the Antichrist"? The dissemination and reception of the *Protocols* is traced in detail, from Russia to the United States, United Kingdom, and France, and especially in Germany. In this context, reference is also made to the controversial assessment of their influence on Hitler and the Nazis. The question of the origins of the *Protocols* is then explored, distinguishing between legends and established facts based on the latest research. Finally, the reception of the *Protocols* today is outlined and the question of the unbroken seductive power of conspiracy thinking is raised.

It is amazing how effective fakes can be. Once published, they take on a life of their own, attracting "believers" and generating further lies and distortions. *The Protocols of the Elders of Zion* (henceforth *Protocols*), first published at the beginning of the twentieth century, have been particularly successful in this respect.[1] Barely noticed at first, after two decades they had been translated into the world's main languages and sold millions of copies. They have become the most influential text of modern antisemitism and the cornerstone of the Jewish-Masonic conspiracy theory. They have spread to all corners of the earth and their "career" is far from over. How could this happen?

At first glance, the text itself seems rather dry, business-like. An unknown Jewish speaker appears in front of an unidentified audience (probably Jews) and explains – in quasi-confessional tones – the secret methods and goals of a supposedly centuries-old Jewish conspiracy against the entire non-Jewish world. The location and time of the meeting are as obscure as the identity of the speaker and his audience.[2] These conspiratorial circumstances and, even more so, the mysterious origin of the *Protocols* have encouraged

DOI: 10.4324/9781003200789-1

speculation and obfuscation, and this not only on the part of their promoters and promulgators but also their opponents and debunkers who, according to Richard S. Levy, "since the 1920s and continuing into the present hour, have created their own set of durable myths concerning the *Protocols*" (Levy 2014: 44). While we can rule out that the *Protocols* are "genuine" – the meeting and the revelation scenario never took place in reality and the text has been proven to be a patchwork of plagiarism and fiction – we still do not know when, where, and with what intention the text was written. It is precisely the fact that the author or authors are not known, but also the emphasized objectivity with which the alleged conspiracy plan is presented point by point, that made it possible for the *Protocols* to be received as an authentic document and make what is described appear "real" in the eyes of their adherents.

The conspiracy plan – strategy, tactics, and objectives

The *Protocols* describe in great detail the strategy and tactics with which the alleged conspirators wish to subvert all areas of political, social, economic, and cultural life and subordinate them to their objectives, using the world association of Freemasons, who are their slaves unto death, for this purpose. The nations are to be ground down by party in-fighting and class struggles, wars and revolutions, economically ruined by the "power of gold" and financial manipulation, infected with the "poison of liberalism" and morally corrupted by rationalism, materialism and atheism – explicit reference is made to the "disintegrating effect" of "Darwinism, Marxism, Nietzscheism" (Anon. 1972: 24).[3] Even a seemingly deep-rooted antagonism like that between capitalists and socialists is in fact part of the common plan of the conspirators, who are both the rulers of the financial markets and the agitators of the working class. Having been shattered and exhausted by anarchy and poverty in this way, the Gentiles, longing for peace and security, will then finally hand over all power to "the Jews" of their own free will.

Upon the ruins of the old social order, the Jewish leaders will then establish – in the guise of legality – a perfectly organized centralist and paternalistic dictatorship headed by a king "of the holy seed of David" (ibid.: 89). This world ruler, chosen and advised by the "Elders", is described as a charismatic father-figure, a model of virtue, self-control, and reason: "The king of the Jews must not be at the mercy of his passions ... [He] must sacrifice to his people all personal inclinations. Our supreme lord must be of an exemplary irreproachability" (ibid.: 88–89). Adored and idolized by the people as a devoted, loving, and kind-hearted father, the Jewish king will rule "with unbending will" over a pacified, unified, and hierarchically ordered world. There will be no room in this world either for the moral corruption engendered by luxury or for the debasing effects of drunkenness, and everyone will have a right – or rather an obligation – to work. Arbitrariness, corruption, and abuse of office will be severely punished: the necessary laws will be short, clear, and cast in stone. In the words of the speaker, who describes himself and his fellow conspirators as "benefactors of mankind":

> We shall contrive to prove that we are benefactors who have restored to the rent and mangled earth the true good and also freedom of the person, and therewith we shall enable it to be enjoyed in peace and quiet, with proper dignity of relations, on the condition, of course, of strict observance of the laws established by us. ... Our authority will be glorious because it will be all-powerful ... Our authority will be the crown of order, and in that is included the whole happiness of man.
>
> (ibid.: 85)

The goal of the conspiracy, as extensively documented in the *Protocols* (more than half of the text is devoted to its description), is therefore not a bloody tyranny of terror or the extermination of the non-Jews,[4] but the establishment of a "new society", a conflict-free "sovereignty of reason" (ibid.: 28). It will be an empire in which the "mass of the people", described as "blind" and incapable of ruling, are completely manipulated, taken care of, and controlled by the State, and live out their lives in dull happiness without having to assume the impossible burden of freedom.[5] Although there is occasional talk of "despotism", this refers less to physical violence and more to a rigid system of punishment and control. It is emphasized that the "inviolability of the person who honourably and strictly observes all the laws of life in common" will be preserved (ibid.: 85). In order to establish this realm of peace and security, sacrifices will, of course, be necessary, but as the speaker is at pains to point out: "the result justifies the means" (ibid.: 19).

It is noticeable that the text of the *Protocols* is completely devoid of the old, traditional accusations against Jews such as deicide, host desecration, well poisoning, ritual murder, blood defilement, fake conversion, or interest taking and usury.[6] The *Protocols* have no relation to the Talmud, the alleged secret anti-Christian book of the Jews, either. Finally, the motives and images of modern, racially motivated antisemitism (such as physical inferiority, financial and sexual greed, racial intermixing) are also lacking. The only clearly anti-Jewish motives and defamations found in the *Protocols* concern the pursuit of world domination, the possession of money and gold, and global networking. On the other hand, there is extensive talk of law and order, a monopoly on violence, state finance and fiscal policy, national economics, the gold standard, higher education, mass media and its control – topics which dominated public discourse at the end of the nineteenth century and are still relevant today.

It is remarkable how rarely the *Protocols*, with their vision of leader cult and mass propaganda, universal surveillance and total subordination, denunciation, control of the legal apparatus, censoring of the press and aspiration to world domination, have been read as an anticipation of the modern police state and related to the totalitarian systems of the twentieth century. This has only happened on a few occasions, for instance, in the work of Hannah Arendt, who in her famous book *The Origins of Totalitarianism* points to the "strangely modern elements" and the "extraordinary actuality" of the *Protocols* (Arendt 1986: 569)[7] which "in their crackpot manner touch on every important issue of the time" (Arendt 1951: 348). And historian Geoffrey Hosking (1997: 394) observed: "Ironically, its [the *Protocol*'s] nightmare vision anticipated features of the Soviet Communist state far more accurately than it described Imperial Russia or the actual organization of the Jews". One can read into the *Protocols* the fear of a dawning modern-totalitarian age, fear of the consequences of industrialization, globalization, and all-encompassing surveillance. The Jewish conspirators then appear as the all-powerful representatives and agents of modernity and become the objects of hatred for modernity's opponents and losers.

The *Protocols* – a negative Utopia

The goal of the Jewish conspirators as depicted in the *Protocols* is the establishment of a worldwide totalitarian welfare dictatorship with socialist features. The Jewish king will ensure social peace and prosperity. For these great services the non-Jews will accept him and worship him as "benefactor". This, however, corresponds to a recurring theme of the famous dystopias in late-nineteenth- and early twentieth-century Russian literature. For instance, we encounter it in "The Grand Inquisitor" in Fëdor Dostoevskii's novel *The Brothers Karamazov* (1879–1880), who – like the speaker of the *Protocols* – deems the majority of human beings weak, immature, and despicable, and relieves them from the burden of freedom in exchange for bread and security (Poliakov 1980: 69–78; Skuratovskii 2001: 193–204). The Jewish emperor of the *Protocols* bears similarities to the Antichrist as sketched by Vladimir Solov'ëv in his *Short Tale of the Antichrist* (1900) (Solov'ëv 1988; Hagemeister 2000, 2010). Solov'ëv's Antichrist is a charismatic "superman" and self-proclaimed "benefactor" (*blagodetel'*), who gains world power with the help of the "mighty brotherhood of the Freemasons" (Solov'ëv 1988: 745) and builds his reign on the promise of universal peace and welfare, by providing "the most basic of all equalities

– the equality of universal satiation" (ibid.: 747).[8] In the same vein, the *Protocols*' Jewish conspirators see themselves as "benefactors", bringing eternal peace and order to the world (Hagemeister 2012b: 81–82, 87). And even in Evgenii Zamiatin's dystopian novel *We* (1920), the vision of a world of harmony and conformity within a united totalitarian "One-State", the all-powerful ruler is known only as "the Benefactor".[9]

However, unlike the literary works cited, in which the critical attitude of their authors is clearly indicated through the way in which the protagonists are presented and the stories told, the *Protocols* lack a narrative or narrated standpoint that could introduce an alternative voice, commenting on the proceedings. At no point is the fictitious speaker's monologue interrupted or broken up. The very artlessness and unemotional, pedantic objectivity with which he describes the plan to conquer the world reinforces the "reality effect", i.e. makes it easier for the reader to believe that this speech is genuine.

"Programme for world conquest" or the "Charter of the Antichrist"

The *Protocols* were first mentioned in April 1902 in an article by Mikhail Men'shikov (1859–1918), a well-known Saint Petersburg journalist and notorious antisemite who dismissed them as an obvious forgery (Men'shikov 2019 [1902]: 286–290). The first documented publication – still incomplete – occurred between August and September 1903 in a series of nine instalments in a small-circulation and short-lived newspaper of the extreme right called *Znamia* (The Banner) in Saint Petersburg.[10] It was entitled *Programme for World Conquest by the Jews*. According to its publisher, the antisemitic publicist and writer Pavel Krushevan (1860–1909), it was a Russian translation of the original French "minutes (or protocols) of a meeting" of the so-called "World Union of Freemasons and Elders of Zion" (Krushevan 1903).

Expanded and amended versions of the *Protocols* appeared under various titles in the revolutionary year 1905 and in the following years in Moscow, Saint Petersburg, and in the Russian provinces; these versions vary considerably not only in the number of sections or "protocols" they comprise and their content, but also as regards the information they provide on their age and origin (De Michelis 2004: 5–22).

The version that was finally to become notorious worldwide – which comprises 24 "protocols" and was supplemented with subheadings, a kind of guide for the reader – is linked to the name of Sergei Nilus (1862–1929). Nilus, a conservative publicist and religious writer, included the *Protocols* in the second edition of his devotional book *The Great in the Small*, published at Tsarskoe Selo in December 1905, to which he then added a new subtitle *And the Antichrist as an Imminent Political Possibility* (Nilus 1905). Nilus said he had received the *Protocols* in 1901 from a friend who had since died. The manuscript, "signed by the representatives of Zion, of the 33rd degree", was supposedly stolen from one of the most highly placed leaders of Freemasonry in France (ibid.: 321–322); later he referred to the "Jewish plan to conquer the world" and claimed that it had been presented by Theodor Herzl at the First Zionist Congress in Basel (Nilus 1917: 88–89).

In his commentary, Nilus interpreted the *Protocols* within the framework of his apocalyptic world-view as the "charter of the Antichrist", a revelatory unveiling of the hidden strategy of the Satanic forces of darkness and their worldly allies – Jews and Masons – in their struggle against the divine forces of light, a struggle which seemed to have entered its final stage at the beginning of the twentieth century (Hagemeister 2012b; see also Chapter 5 in this volume). As a nobleman and (unsuccessful) landowner, Nilus belonged to those victims of rapid modernization and secularization who identified the downfall of their own world with the end of the world in general. In January 1917, a few weeks before the fall of the monarchy in Russia, Nilus

Figure 1.1 Sergei Nilus, ca. 1925. (Private collection M. Hagemeister.)

published the last edition of his book, this time under the dramatic title, *"It Is Near, Even at the Doors": Concerning That Which People Do Not Wish to Believe and Which Is So Near* (Nilus 1917). Nilus regarded the Bolshevik Revolution, which appeared to support the plan of the "Elders of Zion", as the beginning of the reign of the Antichrist, the false messiah of the Jews, who instead of the Heavenly Jerusalem promised paradise on Earth.

For Nilus – and probably also for the pious readers of his books – the "secrets of Judaism", as supposedly revealed in the *Protocols*, had a metaphysical, redemptive-historical meaning (Hagemeister 2018). However, this aspect hardly featured in the subsequent reception of the *Protocols* and their instrumentalization for antisemitic agitation. Jews were no longer seen as actors in the divine plan of salvation, but were now considered in a purely secular light as exponents of a threatening modernity, who destroy traditional ways of life and social orders, and attracted the hatred of culturally pessimistic and socially conservative opponents of modernization. The enemies of Christianity became the enemies of humanity who were employing the latest means of subversion and manipulation in a bid to wrest for themselves secular dominion over the world.

Experiencing crises and searching for a scapegoat – the "triumphal procession" of the *Protocols*

However, in pre-revolutionary Russia the impact of the *Protocols* in the public sphere was extremely limited – especially as they do not deploy any of the traditional Christian anti-Jewish *topoi* – and there is no evidence that they were used on a larger scale to incite hatred and violence against Jews (Levy 2014: 49–50). Even in the course of the biggest anti-Jewish campaign, the sensational ritual murder trial of Mendel Beilis, which took place in Kiev in 1913, the *Protocols* were not even mentioned. Frequently cited reports about the *Protocols* being read out in all 368 Moscow churches or about the Tsar's initially favourable, but later critical comments about them ("Drop the *Protocols*. One cannot defend a pure cause by dirty methods". Cohn 1996: 126; cf. Bronner 2019: 76–78) turn out to be subsequent inventions (Hagemeister 2012c: 150–156).

It was only the upheavals of the First World War, the collapse of the monarchies, the Bolshevik Revolution in Russia, the establishment of the Communist International with the aim of bringing about "world revolution", the economic crises and the ensuing social unrest that created the need for simple explanations and scapegoats; and the *Protocols* suited this purpose perfectly. The Jews' quest for global rule seemed to be the key to understanding the chaos left by the dissolution of the old order. Even opposites, such as Bolshevism and international high finance, were presented as twin characteristics of the Jewish conspiracy. After the Nilus edition was brought to Western Europe and the United States by Russian émigrés to warn of the danger of "Judeo-Bolshevism", the *Protocols* began their "triumphal procession" (Hannah Arendt) across the global stage.[11]

In the United States, the *Protocols* first became public knowledge in 1919, after they had already been circulated the year before in the highest echelons of government. "America was then in the grip of the 'Red Scare', a near hysterical nativist fear of radicalism, anarchism, foreign espionage and subversion, and most of all, the spectre of Bolshevism" (Singerman 1981–1982: 51). In this climate, the *Protocols* appeared in two editions in Boston and New York in 1920. As early as September 1921, Louis Marshall, President of the American Jewish Committee, complained that the *Protocols*

> is [*sic*] distributed in every club, placed in every newspaper. It has been received by every member of Congress and put in the hands of thousands of personalities. It is the topic of conversation in every living room and in every social sphere.
>
> (Poliakov 1985: 248)

Between 1920 and 1927 the industrialist Henry Ford published a series of articles based on the *Protocols* in his high-circulation newspaper *The Dearborn Independent*, claiming that the Jews were using Communism, banking, labour unions, prostitution, gambling, alcohol, the press, the movies, and jazz ("moron music rubbish") to weaken American culture and absorb the United States into a Jewish world government. In February 1921, the *New York World* published an interview with Ford, in which he said:

> The only statement I care to make about the *Protocols* is that they fit in with what is going on. They are sixteen years old and they have fitted the world situation up to this time. And they fit it now.
>
> (Bytwerk 2015: 226)

Some of the articles on the *Protocols* were assembled into a book, *The International Jew: The World's Foremost Problem*. Subsidized by Ford, the book sold more than half a million copies in the United States and was translated into sixteen languages. In 1927, under pressure from the American Jewish Committee, Ford distanced himself from the book and signed a declaration asking his Jewish "fellow-men and brothers" for forgiveness, but it was too late to prevent the spread of this inflammatory document that became an international bestseller. "All in all", historian Norman

Cohn concluded, "*The International Jew* probably did more than any other work to make the *Protocols* world-famous" (Cohn 1996: 174).

The *Protocols* were first published in Great Britain in January 1920 under the lurid title *The Jewish Peril*. The translation was based on the very rare Nilus edition of 1905, a copy of which had come into the possession of the British Museum. It was printed by the King's Printers, Eyre & Spottiswoode. The first edition of 30,000 copies sold out within a few months. In the same year "The Britons", an extreme right-wing organization, published a second and third edition. It was enthusiastically received not only in extremist circles, but also by senior cabinet members and public figures. There was a widespread notion that Bolshevism was the demonic creation of the Prussian military and Jewish financiers seeking to destroy the Empire and take over the world. At the beginning of 1920, the Secretary of State for War, Winston Churchill, who had called for intervention in Russia to "strangle Bolshevism in its cradle", conjured up the spectre of a "deliberate world-wide, profoundly conceived conspiracy" against western civilization in which "atheistical Jews", allied with Bolsheviks in spreading the "gospel of [the] Antichrist", were pursuing a "diabolical plan" to establish tyranny and slavery (Ruotsila 2001: 168, 172, cf. Taguieff 2021: 52–53). Conservative press commentators also shared this view and were inclined to recognize the *Protocols* as genuine. An anonymous reviewer asked anxiously in May 1920 on the front page of the London *Times*:

> What are these "Protocols"? Are they authentic? If so, what malevolent assembly concocted these plans, and gloated over their exposition? Are they a forgery? If so, whence comes the uncanny note of prophecy, prophecy in parts fulfilled, in parts far gone in the way of fulfilment?
> (Anon. 1920: 1)

In France, it was members of the anti-republican Action Française and other right-wing royalist or fascist leagues and Catholic traditionalists that drew attention to the *Protocols*. In October 1920, the influential protonotary apostolic and conspiracy theorist Mgr Ernest Jouin (1844–1932) published the first French translation of the *Protocols* with extensive commentaries both in his journal *Revue Internationale des Sociétés secrètes* and in a separate compendium, *Le Péril Judéo-maçonnique*. Jouin, who was committed to the struggle against "Jewish Freemasonry", "Satan's anti-Church", had extensive contacts with antisemites and opponents of Masonry in many countries. Jouin summed up the distinction frequently made by supporters of the *Protocols* between authenticity and "intrinsic truth" as follows: "Peu importe que les Protocoles soient authentiques; il suffit qu'ils soient vrais"

("It matters little whether the *Protocols* are genuine; it suffices that they are true"; Pierrard 1970: 243).

Russian émigrés had also brought the *Protocols* to Germany, where the population was smarting from the humiliation of defeat in the First World War and were only too happy to attribute the blame to an international Jewish conspiracy and the Jews' alleged striving for world domination.[12] As early as the winter of 1918/19, a number of different versions of the *Protocols* were circulating in nationalist-racist and antisemitic circles in Berlin and Munich. In spring 1919 the Nilus edition of 1911 was translated into German and was published with an extensive commentary in January 1920 as *Die Geheimnisse der Weisen von Zion* (The Secrets of the Elders of Zion) by the antisemitic publicist and agitator Ludwig Müller von Hausen (1851–1926), founder and leader of the sectarian Verband gegen Überhebung des Judentums (League against Jewish Arrogance), using the pseudonym Gottfried zur Beek. Müller's edition was reprinted six times in 1920 alone, and by the time Hitler came to power in 1933, 12 editions had been published. In 1924 Theodor Fritsch (1852–1933), Germany's leading antisemite, prepared from the English edition his own new translation under the title *Die Zionistischen Protokolle. Das Programm der internationalen Geheimregierung* (The Zionist Protocols. The Programme of the International Secret Government).

The *Protocols* and the Nazis – a manual for modern dictators

The *Protocols* began featuring in Nazi propaganda soon after the publication of the first German edition. Their most energetic proponent and advocate was the Baltic German Alfred Rosenberg, the Nazi Party's chief ideologue, who is said to have himself brought a copy of the *Protocols* from Russia to Germany in 1918. "The publication of these Protocols", said Rosenberg,

> has opened the eyes of millions of Europeans … Millions have suddenly found in them an explanation of many otherwise inexplicable phenomena of the present day, which in their essence suddenly no longer seem to be coincidences, but rather the result of covert cooperation between the leaders of classes, parties and peoples ostensibly locked in a bitter struggle: now their secret is out.
>
> (Rosenberg 1923: 3, 5)

Overall, however, the National Socialists' stance on the *Protocols* was inconsistent.[13] Adolf Hitler occasionally mentioned the "Elders of Zion" in his speeches in the early 1920s and expressed his acceptance of the *Protocols* in *Mein Kampf* (1925) on the grounds that "with positively terrifying certainty they reveal the nature and activity of the Jewish people and expose their inner contexts as well as their ultimate final aims" (Bytwerk 2015: 213). Later, too, Hitler used the myth of a Jewish world conspiracy as a propaganda tool, but in so doing he rarely made explicit reference to the *Protocols* in his writing or speaking (Levy 2014: 51–52; Bytwerk 2015: 213). Joseph Goebbels, who continued right to the very end to preach the struggle against Jewish world domination and also used the image of the Jew as "the Antichrist of world history", only spoke sporadically about the *Protocols*, and then invariably with a degree of scepticism. In 1924, he considered them a fake (Bytwerk 2015: 212), while 19 years later he left it open whether they were genuine or "produced by a brilliant contemporary critic" (ibid.: 213). While Julius Streicher's inflammatory weekly *Der Stürmer* frequently quoted the *Protocols* and published a special issue entitled *World Conspirators: The Secrets of the Elders of Zion Revealed* to mark the annual Nazi Party rally in Nuremberg in 1936, Adolf Eichmann claimed that he had never read the *Protocols*; he described the "Elders of Zion" as "fairy tales" (Levy 2014: 55; Hachmeister 1998: 177).

The *Protocols* were repeatedly re-published in Nazi Germany – though they were not, as is often claimed, required reading in all German schools – but public authorities of the Nazi regime always avoided discussing the historical origins of the text. Instead, like Hitler in *Mein Kampf*, they would refer to its "inner truth" (Bytwerk 2015). The question of whether the *Protocols* were authentic was ultimately irrelevant for believers in a Jewish conspiracy. What was crucial was that the *Protocols*' supposed predictions seemed to be borne out by the course of history, thus seemingly giving credence to the notion of puppeteers pulling the strings from behind the scenes.

After 1939, during the "Final Solution to the Jewish Question", the *Protocols* were no longer published in Germany. The reason is unknown. Contemporaries suspected that maybe those in power were afraid that their own methods of ruling and goals invited comparison with those of the Jews allegedly conspiring to conquer the world. Already in the 1930s, critics of the regime had repeatedly pointed out the relationship between the decisions set out in the *Protocols* and the measures taken by the "Third Reich". In May 1935, the independent court expert at the Bern trial, Swiss writer Carl Albert Loosli (1877–1959), had stated in his conclusion that no one adhered to the methods of the so-called "Elders of Zion" better than Adolf Hitler and his government (Hagemeister 2017: 289). In 1936, Alexander Stein (aka Rubinstein, 1881–1948), a socialist refugee from the "Third Reich", had called Hitler a "pupil of the Elders of Zion" in the title of his book (Stein 1936), and in the following year, German émigré writer Iwan

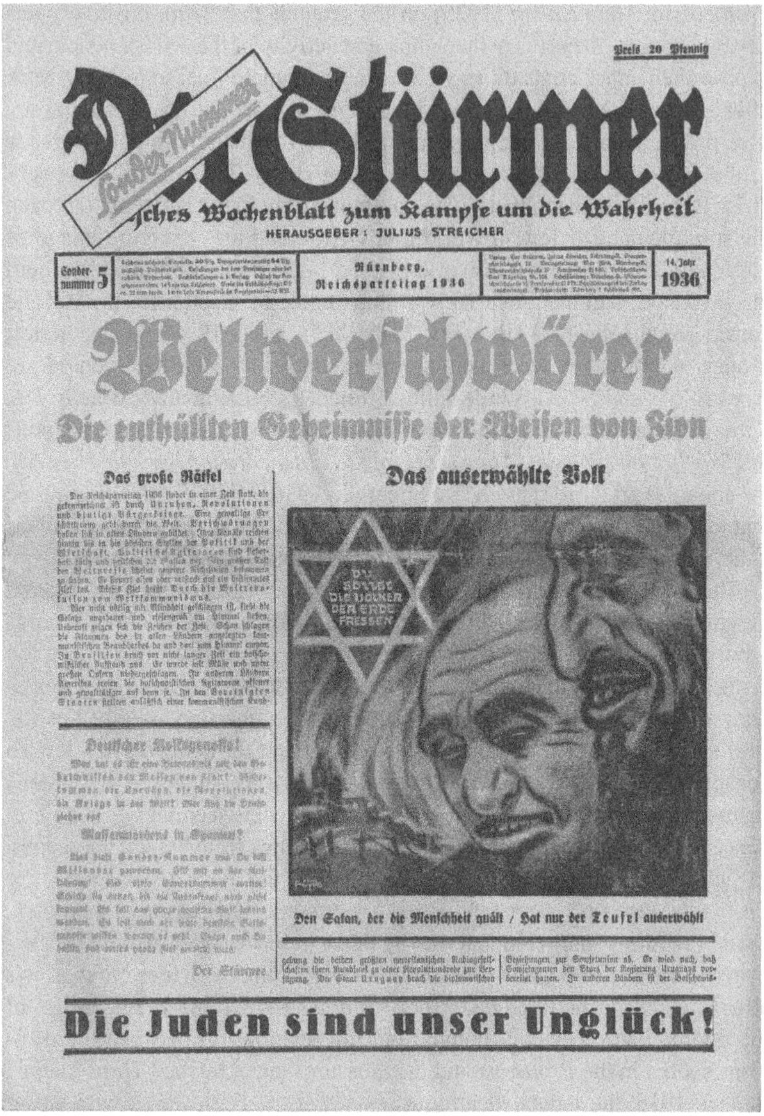
Preis 20 Pfennig

Der Stürmer

Sonder-Nummer

...sches Wochenblatt zum Kampfe um die Wahrheit

HERAUSGEBER: JULIUS STREICHER

Sonder-nummer 5 | Nürnberg, Reichsparteitag 1936 | 14. Jahr 1936

Weltverschwörer

Die enthüllten Geheimnisse der Weisen von Zion

Das große Rätsel

Das auserwählte Volk

DU SOLLST DIE VÖLKER DER ERDE FRESSEN

Den Satan, der die Menschheit quält / Hat nur der Teufel auserwählt

Deutscher Volksgenosse!

Massenmordens in Spanien?

Der Stürmer

Die Juden sind unser Unglück!

Figure 1.2 Der Stürmer. Special edition for the Nuremberg Rally, 1936.

Heilbut (1898–1972), in his pamphlet *Les vrais Sages de Sion*, compared the Nazis' cynical usurpation of power to the alleged plans of world Jewry in the *Protocols* (Heilbut 1937). After the war, Hannah Arendt saw in the *Protocols* a manual for modern dictators and pointed to the ideological similarities between the teachings of the Nazis and those of the "Elders of Zion", noting that: "The Nazis started with the fiction of a conspiracy and modeled themselves, more or less consciously, after the example of the secret society of the Elders of Zion" (Arendt 1951: 366).[14]

The question of what influence the *Protocols* had on Hitler and the Nazis is still intensively debated. Some researchers understood the *Protocols* as a "warrant for genocide" or "license to murder" and established a direct continuity to the Shoah, claiming that "Hitler used the *Protocols* as a manual in his war to exterminate Jews" (Levin 1968: 19). Robert Wistrich (2008: 9), a leading student of antisemitism, believed that "no other single text in the annals of antisemitism has had such a deadly effect as the *Protocols* ... in preparing the Holocaust. ... They profoundly influenced Adolf Hitler and the Nazi Party". Others, like historian Richard S. Levy, considered this an overestimation:

> Are we to believe that he [Hitler; M.H.] needed instruction on the utility of political intrigue, revolutionary disruption, media manipulation, camouflage, diversion, or the ruthless elimination of opponents? These techniques of modern dictatorship were already, or soon would be, stock-in-trade in the interwar years. Conversely, Hitler's personal contributions to the miseries of the twentieth century find few echoes in the *Protocols*. The mass murder, genocide, concentration camps, ethnic cleansing, and interference in the minutest doings of ordinary people carried out on his orders went far beyond the Elders' schemings.
> (Levy 2014: 53–54; see also Hagemeister 2017: 49–53; Evans 2020)

The origins of the *Protocols* – legends and facts

By the end of 1920, translations of the *Protocols* had appeared in Finland, Poland, England, France, Germany and the United States, and numerous other publications appeared in the following years (Thing 2014; Taguieff 2004: 325–342). The various editors and commentators provided more and more new information about the alleged origins, age, and author(s) of the mysterious text. According to them, the *Protocols* document a secret meeting of delegates to the First Zionist Congress held in Basel in 1897, but also of high-ranking French Masons, members of the Grand Lodge "Misraim", the secret organization B'nai Moshe in Odessa, the B'nai-B'rith Lodges, the *Alliance Israélite Universelle*, the Illuminati or the "Central Chancellery of Zion": some asserted that they were connected to the Zionist movement, while others denied this. Authorship has been attributed to Theodor Herzl, Asher Gintsberg (Ahad Ha'am), Adam Weishaupt, and the 12 or 13 or 300 secretive "Elders of Zion", the "secret kings of the Jews". The original text was supposed to have been in French or Ancient Hebrew. Finally, there is the version in which the *Protocols* were written as early as 929 BCE in Solomon's Jerusalem.

Because of the tremendous impact of the *Protocols* and the alarm they caused even to level-headed contemporaries, the question of their origin needed to be clarified urgently. Self-proclaimed witnesses soon appeared, claiming that the *Protocols* had been written in French in Paris by agents of the Russian secret police's foreign agency (Okhrana) and then sent to Russia to combat the modernization and industrialization policies of Russian finance minister Sergei Witte. There is, however, no evidence for this (Ruud and Stepanov 1999: 203–215; Hagemeister 2008a). Recent historical research and textual analysis also denies the existence of an original French version, as well as any involvement of the Russian secret police, and tries to prove that the *Protocols*, in the version distributed worldwide, are a repeatedly overhauled text, written in Russia – more precisely in or around Bessarabia – between 1902 and 1903 as a parody of Theodor Herzl's *Der Judenstaat* (1896), the classic Zionist document, and with reference to the Fifth Zionist Congress (1901) in order to discredit the Zionist movement (De Michelis 2004: 47–49).[15]

It was already established in the early 1920s that the *Protocols* were largely a compilation of literary and journalistic texts. The unknown plagiarists' main source was the work *Dialogue aux enfers entre Machiavel et Montesquieu, ou la politique de Machiavel au XIXe siècle* (Dialogue in Hell between Machiavelli and Montesquieu, or Machiavelli's policy in the 19th century), a witty liberal tract directed against the authoritarian rule of Napoleon III. It was written by the French lawyer Maurice Joly (1829–1878) and first published anonymously in Brussels in 1864 and harks back to a literary tradition of dialogues of the dead; however, while it contains no allusions to Jews, it does refer to the "Machiavellianism" of the Jesuits (De Michelis 1997) and the "Caesarism" of Joseph de Maistre (Battini 2010: 50–58; Ginzburg 2012). An estimated 160 passages, totalling two-fifths of the text of the *Protocols*, had been directly lifted from the *Dialogue* (Segel 1924: 82–114; Anon. 1933), quoting Machiavelli almost exclusively.

Another source was *The Rabbi's Speech*, supposedly delivered to the representatives from the twelve tribes of Israel at the famous nocturnal gathering in the Old Jewish Cemetery in Prague, which was translated into several languages and is based on a chapter in Herrmann Goedsche's (1815–1878) novel *Biarritz* (1868) (Hagemeister 2015b). Undaunted, the adherents of the *Protocols* explained that Goedsche had gained an insight into the "secrets of Judaism" and had published them, in fictional form, while Maurice Joly, secretly a "Hebrew" whose real name was "Moses Joël" or "Joe Levy" (a character in Theodor Herzl's novel *Altneuland*), had himself been a co-conspirator of the "Elders" (Rosenberg 1923: 6; Fleischhauer 1935: 67; Vries de Heekelingen 1938: 10–12). In addition, borrowings from works of nineteenth-century Russian and French popular literature as well as from Fëdor Dostoevskii's novels have been established (Dudakov 1993; Skuratovskii 2001: 191–221).[16]

The question of the "authenticity" of the *Protocols* was also the subject of a court case that took place in Bern between 1933 and 1937, attracting worldwide attention. Drawing on testimonies and documents, the Jewish plaintiffs sought to prove that the text came from the Russian secret police's Paris forgery workshop in the hope that this would break its spell. The history of the origins of the *Protocols* presented in Bern seemed totally convincing and was accepted as definitive for a long time, but a critical historical analysis disproves this account (Hagemeister 2017; see Chapter 2 in this volume). Although the *Protocols* were described in the judgment of the first instance as a plagiarism and a forgery and the court ruled against their Swiss Nazi disseminators, neither the court judgment nor the disclosure of the literary sources were enough to discredit the *Protocols* once and for all.

The seductive power of a conspiracy theory – the *Protocols* today

The work with the misleading title *Protocols of the Elders of Zion* is an "open text" in the sense of Umberto Eco (1990), allowing a variety of different readings (which, of course, does not mean *any* reading). The anti-Jewish interpretation is only one of several, albeit the most widespread. But there are other interpretations. British and American conspirologists explained that the *Protocols* had been written intentionally to deceive and that any reference to Jews should instead be understood as referring to the secret society of the Illuminati (Introvigne 2005: 67–68). Bill Ellis (2005), Professor of English and American Studies, considers it possible that the *Protocols* were "like Taxil's Palladian Freemasonry fabrications, intended to be a spoof, exaggeration the theocratic beliefs of the monarchist minority [in France], particular the Catholic Right by putting them into the mouths of Evil Others". In the international bestseller *The Holy Blood and the Holy Grail*, which inspired Dan Brown's blockbuster novel *The Da Vinci Code* (2003), the *Protocols* form part of the global conspiracy of a secret French

DIALOGUE AUX ENFERS

ENTRE

MACHIAVEL

ET MONTESQUIEU

OU LA POLITIQUE DE MACHIAVEL

AU XIXᵉ SIÈCLE,

PAR UN CONTEMPORAIN.

———

« Bientôt on verrait un calme affreux,
pendant lequel tout se réunirait contre
la puissance violatrice des lois. »

« Quand Sylla voulut rendre la liberté
à Rome, elle ne put plus la recevoir. »
(MONTESQUIEU, *Esp. des Lois.*)

BRUXELLES,

IMPRIMERIE DE A. MERTENS ET FILS,

RUE DE L'ESCALIER, 22.

———

1864

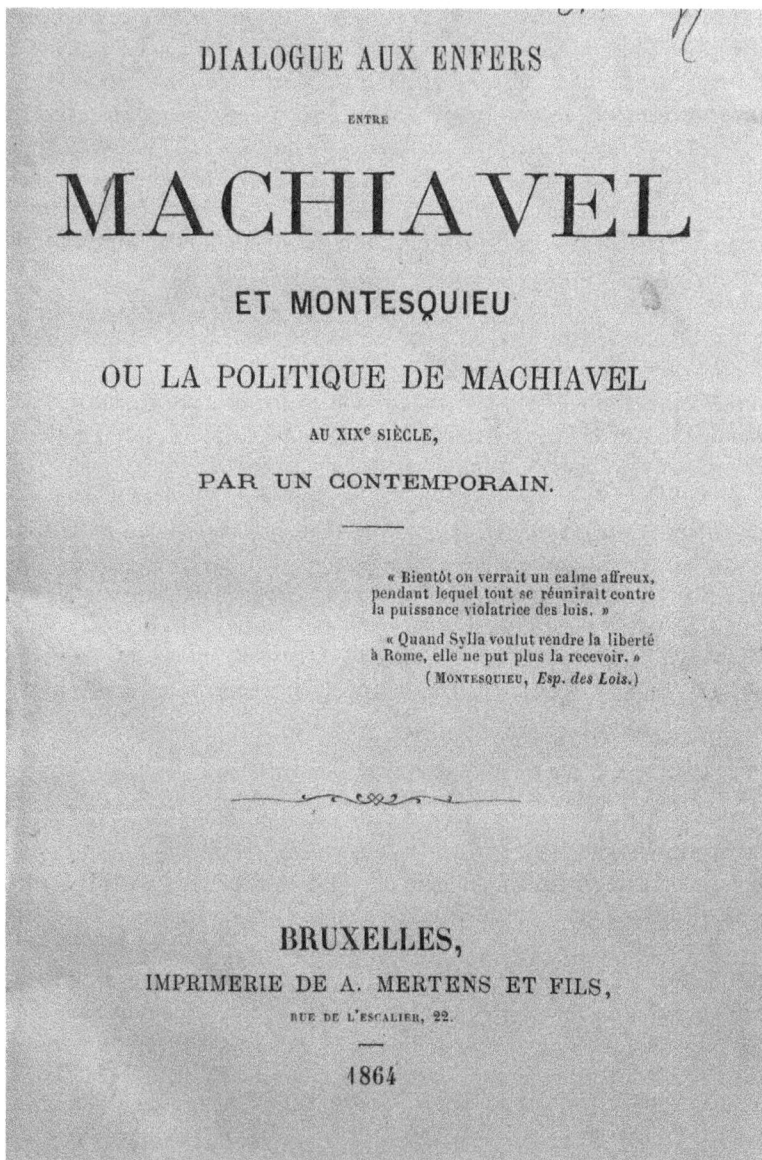

Figure 1.3 Maurice Joly, *Dialogue aux enfers*, 1864.

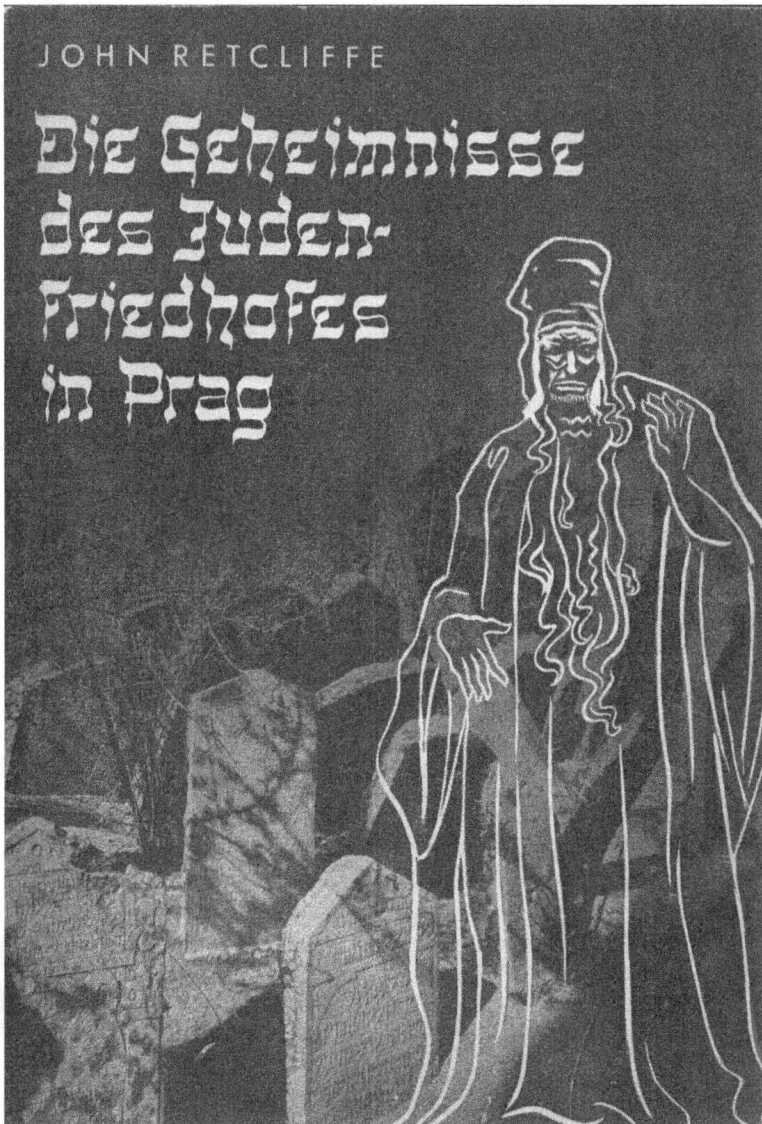

Figure 1.4 John Retcliffe (i.e. Herrmann Goedsche), *Die Geheimnisse des Judenfriedhofes in Prag* (Prague: Orbis, 1942). Cover with an illustration of Rabbi Löw after the statue by Ladislav Šaloun at the New Town Hall in Prague.

order, the "Prieuré de Sion", whose prominent members (including Isaac Newton, Victor Hugo, and Claude Debussy) are attempting to bring the Merovingian dynasty – descendants of Jesus and Mary Magdalene – back to power (Baigent et al. 1990 [1982]: 198–203). For Italian Fascist Julius Evola (1898–1974), the *Protocols* engendered the dream of the "Regnum" – the recreation of the old European supranational Holy Kingdom (Evola 1937). And Aleksandr Dugin (b. 1962), the leading conspiracy theorist in post-Soviet Russia, expressed – following Evola – the opinion that the second part of the *Protocols*, describing the foundation of a sacred monarchy and a caste system, carries the "hallmark of a traditional Aryan mentality" (Dugin 1996: 71; Hagemeister 2015a: 167).[17]

Readers of the *Protocols* are usually influenced by their paratexts, i.e. introductions, headings, and commentaries, which change with each new edition and are usually the most comprehensible part of the whole publication (Horn 2012: 22–24; Kasper-Marienberg 2012: 47–50). The whereabouts of the enemy can vary, depending on the political and social context. At present, the *Protocols* are being distributed worldwide on an unprecedented scale in an endless spate of new editions and are used by the most varied groups, adapting them to their agitation purposes: by Christian fundamentalists and dispensationalists, "White Aryans", "revisionist historians", and "Jew-Watchers" in the United States; by nationalist-patriotic and Orthodox ideologues in Russia; by the Palestinian terrorist organization Hamas in the Middle East; by Holocaust deniers, neo-Nazis, and trash-talking German rappers; by esoteric "New Agers" and by Communists who have replaced the "class enemy" with "Zionist world conspirators"; and, last but not least, by the rapidly growing number of agitators of every ideological stripe on the internet. The geographical reach of the *Protocols* is no longer restricted to Europe, North America, and the Islamic world: readers can also be found in Latin America, South Africa, and even in Japan (Webman 2011).

The fact that their influence is still very much felt today is probably due not so much to their specific content, which in any case is riddled with contradictions, but rather to their material existence, since the *Protocols* purport to prove the existence of a secret plan according to which invisible but omnipotent and omnipresent players manipulate world events as a whole in pursuit of a final goal that is perceived as threatening. Like other "grand narratives", the myth of a conspiracy satisfies the need for a key to understanding and negotiating a threatening, increasingly secular and "disenchanted" world. Impenetrable relationships and anonymous structures are personified so that they become vivid, tangible subjects of a theatre of salvation and damnation: the "enemy" – these are the satanic agents of a worldwide conspiracy, the well-camouflaged, seductive powers of evil that must be exposed and fought. The righteous are implicitly urged to close ranks to repel the enemy.

And finally, the *Protocols* provide comfort by showing that the time of suffering will not last forever and the rule of universal evil will (or can) be overcome. What the *Protocols* have in common with all universal salvation and redemption teachings is that they radically simplify the infinite and confusing nature of reality by reducing it to a one-dimensional, finite, and thus manageable scheme. But this is precisely what shows them to be a fiction.

Notes

1 There is a huge scholarly literature on the *Protocols*. Classic studies are Bernstein (1935), Rollin (1991, 2005 [1939]), Curtiss (1942), and Cohn (1996 [1967]). The most important recent studies are Skuratovskii (2001), a book that deserves to be translated; Taguieff (2004); and De Michelis (2004), of which the original Italian edition (1989) is to be preferred.

2 However, this is not, as the title suggests, a gathering of the "Elders of Zion", since neither the speaker nor the audience are identical with "our elders" occasionally mentioned in the course of the speech. And it is by no means clear from the text that, as is sometimes stated, the *Protocols* "reflect fictitious conversations at a secret conference in the Jewish cemetery in Prague" (Benz 2020: 88) or at a "congress held by representatives from the 'twelve tribes of Israel' and led by a Grand Rabbi" (Bronner 2019: 1). It seems that the *Protocols* are more discussed than read among some scholars.

3 The *Protocols* are distributed in different versions with various titles. I use here the English translation attributed to Victor E. Marsden (former Russia correspondent of the London *Morning Post*) that in most cases closely follows the Russian edition by Sergei Nilus.

4 The English translation of Protocol no. 3, however, suggests this when it says: "We are interested in … the killing out of the goyim". The Russian text here reads *vyrozhdenie*, which means degeneration and is correctly rendered as *Entartung* in the German translation. This is one of the means by which the Jews were to seize power.

5 The characterization of the submissive masses and their relationship to the leader suggests the influence of Gustave Le Bon's epochal work *Psychologie des foules* (1895), which, however, remains to be investigated.

6 Bronner (2019: 1) is therefore wrong when he asserts that the pamphlet "contains many of the most vicious myths about the Jews that have been handed down through the centuries", whereas the claim that "the blood libel" is "central to the *Protocols*" (Glaser 2014: 231) testifies to a complete ignorance of the text. It is precisely the absence of Judeophobic stereotypes that is taken by the defenders of the *Protocols* as proof that the text is authentic and not a crude antisemitic forgery.

7 These quotes only in the German version.

8 This can be understood both as an anti-socialist phrase or as an allusion to the first temptation of Christ (*Mt* 4:3). The *Protocols* also stir up reactionary fears, with the Elders threatening to tax the wealthy heavily and to restrict the production of luxury goods because they corrupt morals (Protocols 22 and 23).

9 Kasper-Marienberg (2012) offers a philologically based reading of the *Protocols* as classical utopia and "satirical criticism of the times". According to Horn

(2012: 12–19), the *Protocols* also stand in the tradition of old European state-craft doctrines (*Staatskunstlehren*).

10 Debunkers of the *Protocols* keep claiming that their first publication had imme-diately inspired the infamous pogrom in Kishinev (Bronner 2019: 61). In fact, the pogrom already took place in April 1903.

11 There is a huge literature on the myth of Judaeo-Bolshevism. See, most recently, Hanebrink (2018).

12 On entanglements between Russian right-wing émigrés and their German like-minded comrades, see Kellogg (2005); Hagemeister (2017: 60–68).

13 Cf. the more recent studies Bytwerk (2015); Taguieff (2020a); Evans (2020). Historian Peter Longerich apparently does not attach any particular importance to the *Protocols* in the Nazi era, as he mentions them in his comprehensive his-tory of antisemitism in Germany briefly only in connection with the antisemitic mass propaganda of the Weimar period (Longerich 2021: 246).

14 Among antisemites, there was also admiration for the art of government of the "Elders of Zion". To the "mastermind of German antisemitism", Theodor Fritsch, they even appeared to be ideal statesmen: "Let us admit that in these Zionist Protocols lies hidden a vast amount of wisdom … If these minds that worked out such things did not pursue special interests that were hostile to soci-ety, they could almost appear to be appointed men to lead a state astutely and with a fine psychological understanding" (Fritsch 1932: 72). Future politicians would have to develop a programme as lucid as the *Protocols*. Fritsch called it the "Aryan Counter-Protocols" (77).

15 It was only in later editions, De Michelis claims, that the *Protocols* were crudely Frenchified in order to make them look more authentic as a foreign document. Recently, however, new arguments have been added to an old assumption that the *Protocols* could have originated in the circle around the French writer and publicist Juliette Adam (1836–1936) (Hillis 2017: 75–78).

16 As early as the 1920s and 30s, antisemites such as Jean Drault (1921) and Herman de Vries de Heekelingen (1938: 10–12) had discovered similarities with literary works by well-known authors – Alexandre Dumas père, Eugène Sue, Sidney Vigneaux and others – but they saw this as evidence of a Jewish world conspiracy tradition in which the *Protocols* participated. Dumas' novel *Joseph Balsamo* (1846) was referred to as the literary precursor of the *Protocols* by René Guénon, Julius Evola and, most recently, Umberto Eco (1994: 134–139).

17 Dugin has (albeit later) condemned theories of a Jewish conspiracy and denied the authenticity of the *Protocols* (Clover 2017: 187).

2 The Protocols of the Elders of Zion in court

The Bern trials 1933–1937

Between 1933 and 1937 a famous court case against the disseminators of *The Protocols of the Elders of Zion* took place in Bern. In fact, the main issue was to prove the authenticity or forgery of the text. To this end, both plaintiffs and defendants attempted to produce a convincing account of the historical origins of the *Protocols*. Based on documents in numerous archives, this chapter traces the preparation, course, and outcome of the proceedings, characterizes the most important people on both sides, and sheds light on the "Antisemitic International" of the interwar period. Although the plaintiffs initially prevailed, the question of authenticity was later deemed irrelevant. More importantly, however, their version of the origins of the *Protocols*, which was canonized at the time, is based, as will be shown, on rather dubious testimonies and does not stand up to historical scrutiny.

> I hope, I don't want to prophecy, I hope a time will come when nobody will understand why in the year 1935 almost a dozen quite sane and reasonable people racked their brains for 14 days before a Bern court over the authenticity of these so-called Protocols, these Protocols which, despite all the harm they have caused and may yet cause, are nothing more than ridiculous nonsense ... With this I shall part from the Protocols stating that: The Protocols are a forgery, they are a plagiarism, and they fall under article 14 of the ... law [against indecent literature].[1]

Walter Meyer (1885–1941), the presiding judge in the case of *The Protocols of the Elders of Zion* quoted above, was mistaken in several respects. First, the case initially heard in the Bern District Court was not over; the defendants appealed and in November 1937, the Court of Appeal overturned Meyer's judgment, declaring that the *Protocols* could not legally be termed indecent.[2] Moreover, the controversy over the *Protocols* continues to this day, and is frequently the subject of legal disputes.

DOI: 10.4324/9781003200789-2

When Meyer pronounced his verdict, the proceedings had already lasted for over a year and a half. At the end of the trial, three of the five defendants accused of disseminating the *Protocols* were acquitted; the other two were fined 20 and 50 Swiss francs, respectively. But this was not the core of the issue.

In their efforts to challenge or defend the authenticity of the text, both plaintiffs and defendants attempted to produce a convincing account of the historical origins of the *Protocols*. Whereas the plaintiffs' version initially prevailed, the question of authenticity was later deemed irrelevant. More importantly, however, their version of the origins of the *Protocols*, based on rather dubious testimonies, does not stand up to historical scrutiny.

In June 1933, the United Jewish Communities of Switzerland (*Schweizerischer Israelitischer Gemeindebund*, SIG) and the Jewish Community (*Israelitische Kultusgemeinde*) of Bern filed a lawsuit in the Bern District Court against the disseminators of the *Protocols*, members and sympathizers of the antisemitic Swiss National Front. The plaintiffs invoked a local Bern law from 1916 referring to "moving pictures and measures against indecent literature [*Schundliteratur*]".[3] Article 14 of the law prohibited "circulating" texts, songs, and images which might incite or instruct someone to commit a crime, endanger good morals, gravely offend one's sense of decency, to exert a brutalizing influence, or "otherwise arouse serious objections". The nominal charge therefore related to the sale of indecent literature. The object, however, was not to punish the Swiss Nazis; rather, it was hoped that proving the *Protocols* were a forgery would disarm the text and thus mean a decisive victory over the intense antisemitism that was especially rampant in Nazi Germany.[4]

In preparation for the trial, the plaintiffs formed a legal committee, with the prominent Bern lawyer Boris Lifschitz (1879–1967) as chair. Originally from Ukraine, he had political reasons for maintaining a discreet distance.[5] Instead, a young lawyer, Georges Brunschvig (1908–1973) took the more public role, since he was, in Lifschitz's words, "an unknown quantity [*ein unbeschriebenes Blatt*]".[6] In June 1934, at a closed legal meeting held in the boardroom of the Jewish community building in Basel, Brunschvig stressed that the *Protocols* formed the basis of the antisemitic movement in Germany and Switzerland. The aim, therefore, was to uncover the "mechanics" of the falsification, and "to reach a verdict", according to which "expertise, witnesses and documents" would demonstrate that the tract was a forgery. Lifschitz added that this public confirmation – and branding – by the Swiss court would be in the "interest of all the Jews".[7] At the same time, it was in the plaintiffs' interest to have a lengthy process during which the other side could state their position in detail. According to Saly Mayer (1882–1950), secretary of the United Jewish Communities of Switzerland and leader of

the Swiss action against antisemitism, in a confidential circular to representatives of the Jewish communities, this would be the only way to ensure
that "an image of complete objectivity" was communicated to the public.[8]
In a further letter to the communities, Mayer called on the representatives
to use their contacts with the press to encourage as much coverage of the
trial as possible.

As the plaintiffs themselves were no experts on Russian matters, they
turned for help within and outside the Soviet Union. An extensive search
in Soviet archives and libraries was coordinated by Aleksandr Tager
(1888–1939), a Moscow lawyer and author of a book on the Beilis affair,
who reported the findings to Bern (Hagemeister 2009a: 134–153; 2017).[9]
Outside the Soviet Union, a search for information was launched by Il'ia
Cherikover (Elias Tcherikower, 1881–1943), a well-known Jewish historian, then living in Paris, author of a book on pogroms in Ukraine during
the Russian Civil War, and one of the founders of the Institute for Jewish
Research (YIVO) in Vilna (now in New York).[10] In less than a year the
plaintiffs managed to collect so many documents that they themselves were
amazed. But together with the "avalanche-like growth" of the materials, as
Lifschitz called it, the costs of the whole procedure exploded. All inform-
ants worked for honoraria (for obtaining the Russian documents alone a
sum of up to 10,000 Swiss francs had been provided), and some of the
witnesses also asked for payment. Nevertheless, the Bern lawyers insisted
on continuing with the investigations. As Lifschitz stated: "we could get
a judgement in our favor immediately without an expert report, but that
would be of no use to us".[11]

During the main hearings, in October 1934 and April–May 1935, the
plaintiffs summoned a wide range of witnesses and experts. These included
several participants in the First Zionist Congress in Basel, the president
of the World Zionist Organization, Chaim Weizmann (1874–1952), and a
number of prominent Russian émigrés, both Jewish and non-Jewish, including Sergei Svatikov (1880–1942), an expert on the Tsarist secret police
abroad; Vladimir Burtsev (1862–1942), an activist and historian of the
Russian revolutionary movement, who had become famous by exposing
a great number of *agents provocateurs*; Boris Nikolaevskii (1887–1966),
another prominent historian and archivist of the Russian revolutionary
movement; Genrikh Sliozberg (1863–1937), a lawyer and Jewish activist; and Pavel Miliukov (1859–1943), former leader of the Constitutional
Democratic Party. All these people were to appear at the trial in Bern as
expert witnesses. Burtsev and Svatikov were financially distressed, while
Nikolaevskii, who had recently fled from Germany, also had financial concerns. Honoraria played an important role in securing not merely their testimony, but their active participation in the search for the origins of the

Protocols. The formula devised by Cherikover to finesse the issue of hono-raria – potentially delicate, since it could be used by Nazi propaganda – was that he was commissioning contributions for a volume of papers and documents on the *Protocols.* This work, for which he asked the Swiss plain-tiffs for the sum of 25,000 French francs, has never materialized, and it is unclear whether Cherikover actually ever intended to complete it.[12]

The plaintiffs' case

The plaintiffs' carefully planned strategy was clear. A unified and plausi-ble story about the origins of the *Protocols* should prove their character as a fabricated, antisemitic concoction. The publicity surrounding the court proceedings would ensure the message reached a wide audience. The plain-tiffs adhered to the version that had begun to be circulated in 1921 by two self-proclaimed witnesses, Catherine Kolb-Danvin (1858–1941), a writer of Russian-Polish origin, who appeared – effectively, albeit illegally – under her divorced husband's name as Princess Radziwill, and the French Count Alexandre Armand de Blanquet du Chayla (1885–1947). The story they told was of a conspiracy of sinister antisemites and reactionaries originating toward the end of the nineteenth century and involving the Tsar's notorious secret police, the Okhrana (Anon. 1921a, 1921b, 1921c; du Chayla 1921a, 1921b, 1921c; Radziwill 1921).

Accordingly, Pëtr Rachkovskii (1851–1910), head of the Okhrana's foreign agency in Paris, a "born intriguer" and ardent Jew-hater, commis-sioned the unsavoury Matvei Golovinskii (1865–1920), a Russian journal-ist and writer living in France, to fabricate an anti-Jewish text. It is in the *Bibliothèque Nationale* that Golovinskii concocts what is to become the *Protocols.* The manuscript, written in poor French and in different handwrit-ings, reached the hands of Sergei Nilus (1862–1929), a mystic and fanatical itinerant preacher in good standing at the Tsar's court. He translated and published the text in 1905 as *The Protocols of the Elders of Zion.* With the help of the Tsar, the *Protocols* were disseminated widely and used to fuel the fires of antisemitic hatred – leading to devastating pogroms in Russia.

Radziwill and du Chayla claimed to have seen the French manuscript from Rachkovskii's forgery workshop with their own eyes. Some aspects of Radziwill's version – she was indeed a notorious swindler[13] – were so obviously fanciful, however, that they met with immediate disbelief and soon disappeared from the discussion.[14] During the Bern trial the American Jewish Committee urgently warned the plaintiffs not to use Radziwill's testimony. Her value as a witness would be "below zero".[15] Du Chayla's account, on the other hand, which was consonant with some elements of

Radziwill's earlier story (which he knew) but omitted her most obvious mistakes, was extremely successful. Lifschitz's team was delighted, particularly since du Chayla had lived in Tsarist Russia for twelve years and had known Nilus personally. Nilus had apparently shown him the French manuscript of the *Protocols* – which in all its details matched the description offered by Radziwill – and confessed that he had received it from Rachkovskii through the mediation of his former mistress ("Madame K."). Overall, du Chayla's depictions of the fanatical Nilus, the sinister machinations of the secret police, and the intrigues and conspiracies of the court, which had all led to the fabrication of the *Protocols*, seemed coherent and persuasive. In addition, they were written in a colourful and enthralling manner, and remain to this day a favoured source, referred to frequently by refuters of the document.[16]

Here is not the place to go into the many factual errors and inconsistencies in du Chayla's story. The important thing is that the narrative had now been shaped into its final version, which could no longer be questioned or changed. The plaintiffs agreed to stick closely to du Chayla's claim that the *Protocols* originated in Rachkovskii's forgery workshop. This version was used as a guideline for the witnesses' statements despite increasing doubts about du Chayla's integrity and the truth of his tale. Boris Nikolaevskii, for example, one of the coordinators on the side of the plaintiffs and an expert on the Tsarist secret police, had come to the conclusion "that Rachkovskii had nothing to do with the writing of the 'Protocols' and could not have had anything to do with it at any point in his career".[17] Du Chayla's description was false; he was a "swindler" (*prokhodimets*), with no idea whatsoever about the origins of the *Protocols*.[18] Nevertheless, Nikolaevskii did not present his findings at the trial, since, as he wrote later, such an action "would have been a stab in the back of the Russian experts, and would have ... put the campaign against Hitler into disarray".[19]

Du Chayla, the principal witness in Bern,[20] appears to have been motivated primarily by financial incentives. Even his sensational accounts of the origins of the *Protocols*, written in 1921, had been produced for a fee. Now he demanded 4,000 Swiss francs to turn up at the trial, a sum which took a great deal of effort for the plaintiffs to raise and almost led to the cancellation of his appearance.[21] What the plaintiffs had no way of knowing, however, was that in Russia, du Chayla had emerged as an antisemite who himself believed in conspiracy theories. During the notorious blood libel trial against Mendel Beilis in Kiev in 1913, he had worked as a journalist for the *Revue contemporaine*, a French-language periodical published in Saint Petersburg and intended as an organ of Russian propaganda in Western Europe. In his articles du Chayla had supported the blood accusation against

Figure 2.1 Pëtr Rachkovskii. (Staatsarchiv des Kantons Bern: BB 15.1.1557e; courtesy of the archive.)

Figure 2.2 Alexandre du Chayla. Source: *Berner Bilderbuch vom Zionisten-Prozeß um die "Protokolle der Weisen von Zion"* (Erfurt: U. Bodung, 1936).

the Jews and called on the "secret leaders of the Jewish nation" to repent (du Chayla 1913; Baran 2008).

The defendants' case

The defendants, who were forced to prove the authenticity of the *Protocols*, had been trying for some time to find an expert witness willing to take the stand. They eventually found Ulrich Fleischhauer (1876–1960), the founder (together with Austrian ex-diplomat Georg de Pottere, 1875–1951) and head of the German private propaganda and news agency *Welt-Dienst* (World Service). This organization, based in Erfurt, was dedicated to "the resolution of the Jewish question" and to the dissemination of the *Protocols*.[22] The "Jewish question" could be "resolved", according to *Welt-Dienst*, through "total Zionism" (*Voll-Zionismus*) – the establishment of a Jewish national state in Madagascar. Fleischhauer, a retired colonel, was a victim of his own conspiratorial obsessions. He decided to counter the "underground Jewish International" with an "Aryan International of Antisemitism," which was equally as conspiratorial as its imagined enemy: It operated with code names and addresses, and sought to create an international network of opposition to Jews.[23]

The Jewish side, however, also succumbed to the temptation of conspiracy theories. They held that Fleischhauer's *Welt-Dienst* was really an "international antisemitic secret society" which, according to the Jewish weekly *Israelitisches Wochenblatt für die Schweiz*, had about 30,000 agents throughout the world (Anon. 1938: 1). *Welt-Dienst* was now being given the opportunity presented by the Bern trial, to crawl out of its (in Brunschvig's words) "subterranean passageways and nesting places".[24] The reality, however, was quite different. *Welt-Dienst* was indeed an industrious "society",[25] but it also had a certain sect-like character, and its international activities were being watched with increasing suspicion by Germany's Gestapo and Security Service. Goebbels' Ministry of Public Enlightenment and Propaganda had initially promised Fleischhauer its support during the Bern trial but withdrew it following an internal report that questioned the authenticity of the *Protocols*.[26] Fleischhauer, who at the time was not a member of the Nazi Party (NSDAP), repeatedly bemoaned the lack of response and backing by officials of the National Socialist state.

An important coordinator on the side of the defendants of the *Protocols* was Nikolai Markov (1866–1945), leader of the extreme right in Tsarist Russia and, after the Revolution, in Berlin and Paris. In 1935 he moved to Erfurt and became an associate of Fleischhauer in *Welt-Dienst*. In order to collect information about the origins of the *Protocols*, the authenticity of which he did not question, Markov began an extensive correspondence among like-minded compatriots. This documentation, scattered among various archives in Russia, Western Europe, the United States, and Israel, represents a kind of "Who's Who" of Russian far-right émigrés. Among Markov's correspondents were the former Cossack ataman and prolific novelist Pëtr Krasnov (1869–1947), the antisemitic publisher Prince Mikhail Gorchakov (1880–1961), the former head of the Okhrana general Aleksandr Spiridovich (1873–1952), the anti-Masonic author Nikolai Stepanov (1886–1981), who wrote under the pseudonym "Svitkov" and ended up in Palestine as monk Aleksandr, and the antisemitic writer Aleksandr Nechvolodov (1864–1938), all living at that time in Paris, as well as Pëtr Shabel'skii-Bork (1893–1952) and Sergei Taboritskii (1895–1980) in Berlin, the enigmatic blood-libel propagandist Eugen Brandt (Evgenii Brant, 1889–1941) in Copenhagen, Nikolai Zhevakhov (1875–1945) in Bari (Italy), and Prince Anatol Lieven (1872–1937), a member of the anti-Communist "Brotherhood of Russian Truth", to name only the most prominent ones.

Even if the Russian émigrés seemed to be particularly competent in the dispute over the origin of the *Protocols* and provided the majority of the witnesses named by the defence, they were not the only ones on whose support Fleischhauer and de Pottere could count. They were joined by other members of the "Antisemitic International", such as the French *conspirationnistes* from the circle around Ernest Jouin (1844–1932) and the *Revue Internationale des Sociétés secrètes*, or the go-getting but extremely discreet American Leslie Fry (1882–1970). In the course of inquiries, it became known that Pëtr Rachkovskii's son Andrei (1886–1941) was living in Clamart near Paris and had kept his father's extensive archive. As a result, both opponents and supporters of the *Protocols* tried to get hold of these documents. One critic of the *Protocols*, Henri Rollin (1885–1955), who wrote an important study on this subject (Rollin 1991, 2005 [1939]), even tried to buy the entire archive from Andrei, whose sympathies, however, were apparently on the side of the supporters. The latter convinced him to issue a statement in which he confirmed that his father had played no part in the process of concocting the *Protocols*.[27]

Trial proceedings and aftermath

The proceedings at the Bern District Court lasted over a year and a half and caused, thanks to the intensive news coverage, an international sensation. The Jewish Central Information Office (JCIO) in Amsterdam produced a detailed daily information bulletin.[28] By far the majority of Swiss and international news publications declared outright support for the Jewish plaintiffs. In addition to their rejection of the *Protocols*, their views were influenced in large part by the arrogant, intransigent manner of the German "expert on Jews and Freemasons", Fleischhauer. His "expert report" – to a large extent produced by his staff (nicknamed the "Elders of Erfurt") under the guidance of Hans Jonak von Freyenwald (1878–1953),[29] a retired Austrian civil servant and "professional" antisemite – was a meandering, long-winded, and unintelligible composition filled with a potpourri of antisemitic stereotypes.[30] By the end of his four-and-a-half-day appearance in court, Fleischhauer, and thus the defenders of the *Protocols*, had publicly dismantled their own arguments.

The plaintiffs, on the other hand, had apparently managed to prove, without a shadow of a doubt, the origins of the *Protocols*. Their strategy turned out to be a resounding success. On 14 May 1935, trial judge Walter Meyer ruled that the tract was a forgery and a plagiarism, largely based on Maurice Joly's political pamphlet *Dialogue aux enfers entre Machiavel et Montesquieu ou la politique au XIXe siècle* (published anonymously in 1864 in Brussels), and that its dissemination contravened the Bern law on

Figure 2.3 Ulrich Fleischhauer, expert witness for the defence. (Courtesy of Archiv für Zeitgeschichte, Zurich.)

indecent literature. Two members of the National Front were sentenced to a small fine, but to pay a large part of the high costs. The plaintiffs welcomed the verdict as a victory in the campaign against Nazi antisemitism and designated the trial as the most significant "defensive battle" in the history of the United Jewish Communities of Switzerland. For the first time, declared the JCIO, the judiciary had officially branded the *Protocols* a forgery.

The German Nazis did not seem too unsettled, however. Even before the proceedings had ended, the NSDAP newspaper *Völkischer Beobachter* stated categorically that the verdict was quite irrelevant. More importantly, "the entire history of the preceding three decades has unfolded perfectly in line with the Jewish plan described in the *Protocols*" (Siewert 1934). The vehement fight against the *Protocols* only proved that "the Jews" were in fact pursuing a secret plan of world domination, the exposure of which was to be prevented by all means. *Deutsche Juristen-Zeitung*, edited by Carl Schmitt, dubbed the "crown jurist of the Third Reich", also paid the verdict no heed. No legal decision could halt the course of history; the final verdict would be decided by history: "Trials that anticipate a historical decision are inevitably lost by the judiciary" (Anon. 1934: 1465).

Figure 2.4 (From left to right) Judge Walter Meyer, Arthur Baumgarten, expert witness for the plaintiffs, and Carl Albert Loosli, independent court expert. (Courtesy of Archiv für Zeitgeschichte, Zurich.)

The Jewish plaintiffs were therefore sorely disappointed when on 1 November 1937 the Bern Court of Appeal (*Obergericht*) overturned the 1935 judgment. It ruled that the *Protocols* were indeed trash literature in the aesthetic, literary sense, but not as defined by the law since the text had no moral or ethical impact but was political propaganda. Prosecutor Robert Loder had even called them "inflammatory writing" and "outrageous piece of work" and appealed to the legislator to take measures against the dissemination of such writings. The existing law, on the other hand, to which the judge was bound, was not sufficient for a conviction. The question of authenticity was thus deemed irrelevant and dissemination of the *Protocols* not a criminal offence. The defendants were acquitted and the costs of both trials, some 28,000 Swiss francs, were deducted from state coffers.[31]

After analyzing the 50-page report detailing the grounds for the new ruling, prominent Swiss lawyer David Farbstein (1868–1953) – himself a participant in the First Zionist Congress and a witness at the Bern trial – strongly advised against criticizing the decision. No principles of law had been breached. The defendants had to be acquitted since it was unreasonable

Figure 2.5 The courtroom in Bern. (Courtesy of Archiv für Zeitgeschichte, Zurich.)

to expect them to notice what not even the judge could see despite the aid of a lengthy report – that the *Protocols* were a forgery.[32]

Fleischhauer and *Welt-Dienst* celebrated the Appeal Court verdict as if they themselves had won. But their elation was short-lived. In 1939 *Amt Rosenberg* (the Nazi organization under the command of Alfred Rosenberg) took over *Welt-Dienst*, moved its archive to Frankfurt, and replaced Fleischhauer as head. The staff who, according to Adolf Eichmann, were "pretty dubious characters",[33] were all fired. Fleischhauer himself disappeared from the scene.[34] A planned 8–13 volume edition of the files and reports of the Bern trials by Jonak von Freyenwald was also cancelled in 1939 after only the first volume appeared (Jonak von Freyenwald 1939). The era of bizarre idiosyncratic conspiracy theorists was over; the time was ripe for pragmatic, professional practitioners of power.

The Bern trials leave an ambivalent impression. The narrative employed by the plaintiffs in their attempt to uncover the origins of the *Protocols* was a dubious construction, based on equally dubious witnesses – a fact of which at least some of those involved were aware. This narrative had now been authorized by a legal court. All that was left was to publicize it. This is where Henri Rollin comes in. In 1939 his book *L'Apocalypse de notre temps* appeared in Paris (Rollin 1939).[35] The book allowed the French journalist and secret service officer to develop his view of the conspiracy between German and Russian antisemites, who, from their bases in Berlin and Munich in the 1920s and 30s, spread the myth of the Jewish-Bolshevik global conspiracy, and – more or less consciously – made use of a forgery to do so. Basically, Rollin produces an anti-myth, in that the German-Russian antisemitic conspiracy he uncovers is almost identical to the Jewish conspiracy.

Another contribution to the conspiracy narrative surrounding the *Protocols* is from Konrad Heiden (1901–1966). His famous book *The Fuehrer: Hitler's Rise to Power* (1944) describes in the opening chapter the scene in which Alfred Rosenberg, who later became the leading ideologue of the Nazi movement, is passed the *Protocols*.

> One day in the summer of 1917 a student was reading in his room in Moscow. A stranger entered, laid a book on the table, and silently vanished. The cover of the book bore in Russian the words from the twenty-fourth chapter of Matthew: "He is near, he is hard by the door." – The student sensed the masterful irony of higher powers in this strange happening. They had sent him a silent message. He opened the book, and the voice of a demon spoke to him.
>
> (Heiden 1944: 1)

This story turns Rosenberg into a tool of the antisemitic conspiracy and is of course impossible to verify (Levy 2014: 52–53). In fact, it paraphrases a story told by Philip Graves, the Istanbul correspondent for the London *Times*, in which he tells of the mysterious "Mr X" who gave him a copy of Maurice Joly's anti-Napoleonic pamphlet in August 1921, which allowed him to expose the *Protocols* as plagiarism (Graves 1921).[36]

In 1967 a book was published which for a long time became the standard reference for the *Protocols*: Norman Cohn's *Warrant for Genocide* (Cohn 1996 [1967]).[37] Basically, Cohn did no independent research, preferring to compile the findings of others. Most of these stemmed from Boris Nikolaevskii. Although this is not clear from Cohn's book itself (which was published after Nikolaevskii's death and does not reveal his contribution), it is apparent in the correspondence between Nikolaevskii and Cohn's Russian wife, Vera, from 1964 to 1966, which is available at the Hoover Institution in Stanford. As already mentioned, Nikolaevskii was convinced that the origins of the *Protocols* had nothing to do with Rachkovskii and the Okhrana, and that the key witness for that narrative, Alexandre du Chayla, was a "swindler". It was time, he wrote, to abandon the accusations against Rachkovskii, as they stood in the way of researching the *Protocols*. Nevertheless, Norman Cohn held onto du Chayla and his tale.

The reason for this deserves to be quoted: "Of course", wrote Vera Cohn to Nikolaevskii, du Chayla was indeed a "swindler", but his description was so "picturesque" (*zhivopisno*) that "it would be a shame to omit it".[38] Du Chayla's Okhrana tale then figures in key passages of Cohn's book and delivers the "facts" which even today strongly determine the narrative of the origins of the *Protocols*. Enthralling and effective as it is, there is little doubt that this narrative contributed to the myth surrounding the *Protocols* and thus to its success.

The Bern trials are also the topic of Hadassa Ben-Itto's *The Lie That Wouldn't Die* (2005). The author, a prominent judge and diplomat from Israel, wrote her book "for people who want to know what really happened" (Ben Itto 1998: 10). The result is a peculiar mix of fact and fiction, largely based on Cohn, a kind of historical novel with invented episodes, dialogues and inner monologues. Despite its limited scholarly value, the book was enormously successful among critics and has been translated into ten languages. A quote from the advertising blurb for the German edition:

> The "Jewish global conspiracy" is still used today to explain wars and revolutions, economic crises and stock market crashes, terrorism and AIDS. Again, and again the threads come together in a book: the *Protocols of the Elders of Zion*. Hadassa Ben-Itto gets to the bottom of the story of these *Protocols* over seven years of research. The result is a factual report which could not be more absorbing and enthralling if it were invented, although the subject matter would make an ideal thriller: conspiracy and murder, princesses and the Russian imperial family, secret services and leading industrialists – and a virtuous young lawyer, who takes on all of this.[39]

There's really nothing to add to this description. We are by now far from historical research, moving in the realms of conjectural history and pure fiction: exciting, lively stories which can be relayed well even in a comic book. In the graphic novel *The Plot: The Secret Story of the Protocols of the Elders of Zion* – for which Umberto Eco wrote the introduction – the well-known cartoonist Will Eisner traces, in good faith, the "true history" of the *Protocols* (Eisner 2005; see Chapter 5 in this volume). It is the tale originally told by Catherine Radziwill and Alexandre du Chayla and subsequently legitimized by the Bern trials (Hagemeister 2008a).

Conclusion

When dealing with the history of the *Protocols*, one often comes to the border between fiction and factuality, and can observe how this borderline is crossed. The *Protocols* were compiled from a series of fictional texts and then presented as the authentic document of an actual conspiracy. But the literature *about* the *Protocols* also far too frequently ignores the border between fact and fiction, when, for example, comprehensive and (admittedly) gripping *stories* take precedence over well-researched *histories*. We still do not know by whom, when, and for what purpose, the *Protocols* were fabricated. What we hear is a narrative, to be precise a conspiracy narrative. But the actors this time are not Jews, but cunning secret agents, fanatical antisemites, and sinister reactionaries. The myth of the Jewish conspiracy has been responded to with a counter-myth, which is no less mysterious than that which it aims to counter. This shows that the critics of the conspiracy myth also too easily succumb to the seductive power of what they are trying to overcome. As the history of the *Protocols* indicates, the concept of conspiracy offers clear answers when in reality the relations are complex and opaque. Perhaps we will never discover the origins of the *Protocols*. But that should only be frustrating for a handful of historians. Everyone else already knows all too well what they want to believe.

Notes

1 Stenographic protocol of court proceedings, 14 May 1935, Staatsarchiv des Kantons Bern, Bern (StAB): BB 15.1.1557 a.
2 For a detailed description of the Bern trials (1933–1937) – often misleadingly referred to as the "Zionist trial" (*Zionistenprozess*) – and publication of the most important documents, see Hagemeister (2017); for a concise depiction, see Lüthi (1992).
3 The German term *Schund* can mean trashy, smutty, obscene, or indecent. For the purposes of this chapter, the word "indecent" will be used.
4 A trial which was already under way against disseminators of the *Protocols* in Basel was deferred in favour of the Bern trial. Since the canton of Basel had no law against the dissemination of indecent literature, this case involved a libel suit (*Ehrbeleidigung*). The action had been brought by three well-known Jewish leaders, Jules Dreyfus-Brodsky (1859–1942), president of the Jewish Community of Basel; Marcus Cohn (1890–1953), president of the Swiss Zionist Federation; and Marcus Ehrenpreis (1869–1951), chief rabbi of Stockholm. The proceedings in Basel ended in July 1936 with a settlement (Hagemeister 2017: 413–447).
5 In 1918 Lifschitz had worked as legal advisor to the Soviet mission in Switzerland. In 1921 he became a member of the Communist Party, and in 1924 he switched to the Social Democratic Party. From 1933 to 1950 he was consul of Nicaragua and on friendly terms with the dictator Anastasio Somoza García. In 1949 he became Minister Plenipotentiary of the then Communist-ruled Republic of San Marino in the Principality of Liechtenstein with a bogus domicile in Vaduz. Since 1916, Lifschitz was on file with the Office of the Attorney General of Switzerland (extensive personal dossier in Federal Archives, Bern) and was

observed suspiciously by the Swiss authorities as a "salon Communist" until his end.

6   Boris Lifschitz to Helene Lifszyc, 31 May 1935, Wiener Collection, University of Tel Aviv (WC): Bern Trial, box 28. The two other members of the legal committee were the Bern lawyers Walter Bloch (1897–1971) and Willy Hirschel (1900–1958).

7   Protocol of a meeting of the legal committee, 1 June 1934 (note: "strictly confidential"), in Archiv für Zeitgeschichte (AfZ), Zurich: IB SIG Berner Prozess, box 30. The Jewish plaintiffs were accused by their antisemitic opponents and by a number of Swiss newspapers of solely using the court for their case, namely to prove the spuriousness of the *Protocols*. Werner Ursprung, lawyer of the defendants, to the judge's office, 28 November 1933, StAB: BB 15.1.1557 b, 117–119.

8   Saly Mayer, letter of 2 November 1934, AfZ: IB SIG Berner Prozess, box 76. On Saly Mayer and his role in the Bern trials, see Zweig-Strauss (2007: 66–68).

9   Most of the correspondence between Tager and the plaintiffs is kept in AfZ: IB SIG Berner Prozess, box 174, see also boxes 150, 162, 177, 179, 197. Hagemeister (2017).

10 Cherikover's extensive correspondence is kept in the Tcherikower Archives, YIVO Institute, New York, the Bakhmeteff Archive, Columbia University, New York (Svatikov Collection), the Hoover Institution, Stanford (Boris I. Nicolaevsky Collection), AfZ (SIG papers), and the Wiener Collection Tel Aviv). I wish to thank Henryk Baran (University at Albany) for information on the New York archives.

11 Protocol of a meeting of the legal committee, 1 May 1934, AfZ: Nachlass Philippe Schwed, box 2.

12 Protocol of a meeting of the plaintiffs with Cherikover, Svatikov, Sliozberg, and Nikolaevskii, Paris, 13–15 January 1934, AfZ: Nachlass Philippe Schwed, box 2. All that came out was a small *étude* by Cherikover, "Les 'Protocoles', leur origine et leur diffusion" (ca. 1935), a manuscript of 36 pages, which went unpublished, but is kept in AfZ: IB SIG Berner Prozess, box 56 (Russian version, box 61). Burtsev (1938) later published a book on the *Protocols* and the Bern trial.

13 The French writer André Maurois branded her a "mythomaniac", in whose life "everything was only deception and lies" (Maurois 1981: 761, 763). For biographical details, see Aronov et al. (2009); Hagemeister (2012a).

14 In several sensational articles Radziwill had exactly described how Golovinskii visited her in the winter of 1904/1905 in her apartment on the Champs-Elyseés and proudly presented her with the French manuscript of the *Protocols*, which he had just prepared according to Rachkovskii's orders. What Radziwill did not know, however, was that the *Protocols* had already been published in 1903 in Russia. And, of course, she never had an apartment on the Champs-Elyseés. Already a few weeks after the publication of Radziwill's statements, Vladimir Burtsev (1921) pointed out the numerous factual errors, which earned him the reproach in the liberal press of working into the hands of the antisemites with his criticism. Radziwill, who died in poverty in New York in 1941, never referred to her story again. Golovinskii's name came up once again in the autumn of 1999 when the world press sensationalized the fact that the Saint Petersburg literary scholar Mikhail Lepekhin had uncovered him as the author of the *Protocols*

(Hagemeister 2008a: 83). Although he never produced any evidence, the previously unknown Lepekhin became a "leading Russian historian" overnight.

15 American Jewish Committee to Alfred Wiener, 16 February 1934; Alfred Wiener to George Brunschvig, 25 February and 2 March 1934, AfZ: Nachlass Philippe Schwed, box 3.

16 The French expert on the *Protocols* Pierre-André Taguieff (2004: 41) called du Chayla's testimony on Sergei Nilus and the origins of the *Protocols* "certainly most important and trustworthy". The personality of du Chayla is still shrouded in mystery. In the 1930s he lived as a journalist in Suresnes near Paris and in a village in the Savoy Alps. After the occupation of France by the Wehrmacht, his papers were confiscated and taken to Berlin for evaluation by the Reich Main Security Office (*Reichssicherheitshauptamt*). In 1945, they fell into the hands of the Red Army, were brought to Moscow and kept hidden in a secret Special Archive (*Osobyi arkhiv*). After this archive was opened, I was able to view them in 1993. In the meantime, they belong to the holdings of the State Military Archives in Moscow and are closed for use.

17 Boris Nikolaevskii to Vera Cohn, 30 August 1964, The Boris I. Nicolaevsky Collection, Hoover Institution, Stanford (BNC): series 11, box 20, folder 24. Boris Nikolaevskii to Boris Lifschitz, 10 August 1937, AfZ: IB SIG Berner Prozess, box 57.

18 Boris Nikolaevskii to Vera Cohn, 15 August 1964, BNC: series 11, box 20, folder 24.

19 Boris Nikolaevskii to Vera Cohn, 30 August 1964, ibid.

20 Lifschitz labeled du Chayla "our crown witness" (*unser Kronzeuge*); protocol of a meeting of the legal committee, Bern, 27 August 1934, AfZ: Nachlass Philippe Schwed, box 2. Du Chayla himself was quite aware of his importance: "je suis le seul témoin réel, le seul qui a vu" (I am the only real witness, the only one who has seen), he wrote to Lifschitz, 2 May 1935, AfZ: IB SIG Berner Prozess, box 178.

21 Du Chayla to Sergei Svatikov, 7 June 1934, YIVO Institute Archives, New York: Tcherikower Papers. For more on the difficult negotiations between du Chayla and representatives of the plaintiffs, see Hagemeister (2017).

22 Contact was arranged by Boris Tödtli (1901–1944), a Swiss fascist and antisemite born in Russia. A request to the Brown House in Munich, the national headquarters of the Nazi Party, to furnish the defence with an expert witness, was unsuccessful. On Tödtli, see Williams (1969), Hagemeister (2017: 576–577).

23 On Fleischhauer and *Welt-Dienst*, see Brechtken (1997: 43–61, 68–74), Hagemeister (2017: 73–78).

24 Raas and Brunschvig (1938: 45). Nikolaevskii (1935: 731) also considered *Welt-Dienst* to be an antisemitic "central office" which had significant resources and covered "all antisemitic organizations as well as those close to the antisemites". It had succeeded in "bringing almost the entire antisemitic press of the world under its influence".

25 Strictly speaking, *Welt-Dienst* was not even a registered society, but a loose international alliance of like-minded persons.

26 See Heiber (1966: 1062–1063). Rogge (1961: 76) argues the opposite – without documentation: Fleischhauer admitted ("he … told us") after the war that he had received 30,000 Marks from the Ministry of Propaganda for the Bern trials.

27 Témoignage de A.P. Ratschkowsky pour le procès de Berne, 1936, AfZ: IB SIG Berner Prozess, box 57. Andrei Rachkovskii died in March 1941 in Southern

France. The fate of his father's archive is uncertain and the various statements concerning its whereabouts are contradictory. While Nikolaevskii claimed that Rachkovskii's archive had been sold to the German antisemites from *Welt-Dienst* and had obviously been lost, the Saint Petersburg literary scholar Mikhail Lepekhin stated in an interview for French television in 2007 that in 1936 it had been stolen on Stalin's orders by GPU agent Iakov Serebrianskii (aka Bergman).

28 The Jewish Central Information Office, founded in June 1934 by Alfred Wiener (1885–1964) and David Cohen (1882–1967), supplied the plaintiffs in Bern and Basel with rare books and materials and carried out investigations. Its main task, however, was to report on the situation of Jews in Germany and on antisemitic movements throughout the world.

29 Ubald von Roll to Princess Mary Karadja, 5 February 1935, AfZ: IB SIG Berner Prozess, box 75; von Roll, head of Bern district (*Gauführer*) of the National Front, quotes Jonak von Freyenwald's pen-name "Dr. Richter."

30 The report, for which he received 8,000 Swiss francs from the court, was published: Fleischhauer (1935).

31 Protocol of the appeal process, 1 November 1937, StAB: BB 15.1.1557 d.

32 David Farbstein to Saly Braunschweig, 7 March 1938, in AfZ: IB SIG Berner Prozess, box 70. In contrast to most commentators on the judgement, Sibylle Hofer, professor for Legal History at the University of Bern, agrees with the Court of Appeal's criticism of the first-instance proceedings. The judgement of the District Court judge was essentially based on political views and less on strictly legal application of the law. In contrast, she evaluates the decision of the higher court in a precise legal analysis as a defence of central principles of the rule of law (Hofer 2011a, 2011b).

33 Eichmann quoted in Brechtken (1997: 69).

34 After the war Fleischhauer fled to West Germany. He lived on welfare in Hürben near Heidenheim. Until his death in October 1960 he kept contact with former collaborators of *Welt-Dienst* and experts for the "Jewish question", among them Mahmoud Saleh (1909 – after 1977), who headed the Institute for the Study of Zionism in el-Maâdi near Cairo.

35 A legend still circulating today is that Rollin's book, published by Gallimard, is very rare because it was confiscated by the Nazis during the occupation of France and destroyed. The book actually went through eight editions in 1939, was widely available and can still be found in second-hand bookshops.

36 The identity of "Mr X" – Mikhail Raslovlev (1892–1987), a Russian nobleman and monarchist – was already known to the plaintiffs in the Bern Trial in the mid-1930s but kept secret until 1977.

37 Richard S. Levy (2014: 54–55, 61) criticizes the title. Although Cohn considers the *Protocols* responsible for the massacres in the Russian Civil War and the main cause of the Holocaust, he has not succeeded in proving this.

38 Vera Cohn to Boris Nikolaevskii, 23 August 1964, The Boris I. Nicolaevsky Collection, Hoover Institution, Stanford (BNC): series 11, box 20, folder 24.

39 Advertising brochure of Aufbau-Verlag Berlin, 1998, 24.

3 On the early history of *The Protocols of the Elders of Zion*

The lost copy of the Lenin Library

This chapter follows the multiple traces of an early handwritten copy of *The Protocols of the Elders of Zion*. During the Bern trial in the 1930s, photocopies of the mimeographed manuscript, which was then in the possession of the Lenin Library in Moscow, were sent to the plaintiffs. Later enquiries about this manuscript, however, remained unsuccessful. The search for the earliest handwritten editions of the *Protocols*, especially in Russian emigrant circles, is described in detail. In particular, the question of whether the (lost) Moscow manuscript represents the handwritten copy of the *Protocols* mentioned in Filipp Stepanov's famous affidavit from 1927, a central testimony to the history of the text's creation, is explored.

Stepanov's affidavit

In April 1927 Filipp Petrovich Stepanov, a Russian émigré living in Yugoslavia, made the following handwritten affidavit:

> In 1895 my estate neighbour in the government of Tula, retired Major Aleksei Nikolaevich Sukhotin, gave me a handwritten copy of the "Protocols of the Elders of Zion". He told me that a lady he knew (but whose name he did not give me), when residing in Paris had found them at the home of a friend of hers (I think he was a Jew) and before leaving Paris, had translated them without his knowledge. She had brought a single copy of this translation to Russia and given it to him – Sukhotin.

> At first I made a hundred copies of it with a hectograph (*na khektografe*), but this edition proved difficult to read, and so I decided to have it printed at a printing house, without specifying the year, the place and the printing house. I was helped in this by Arkadii Ippolitovich Kellepovskii [sic], who at the time was an official for special duties to the Grand Duke Sergei Aleksandrovich. He had them printed in

DOI: 10.4324/9781003200789-3

the Governorate Printing Office; this happened in 1897. S.A. Nilus reprinted these protocols in his book and added his comments.

Filipp Petrovich Stepanov, former Procurator of the Moscow Synodal Office, Chamberlain, Active State Councillor, at the time of that edition district head of the line service (in the town of Orël) of the Moscow-Kursk railway.

Underneath it was written by another hand:

I hereby confirm the signature of the member of the colony of Russian refugees in Stari and Novi Futog (Kingdom of Serbs, Croats and Slovenes). Stari Futog, 17 April 1927.

The chairman of the colony administration Prince Vladimir Golitsyn.

(Fry 1934a: 89)

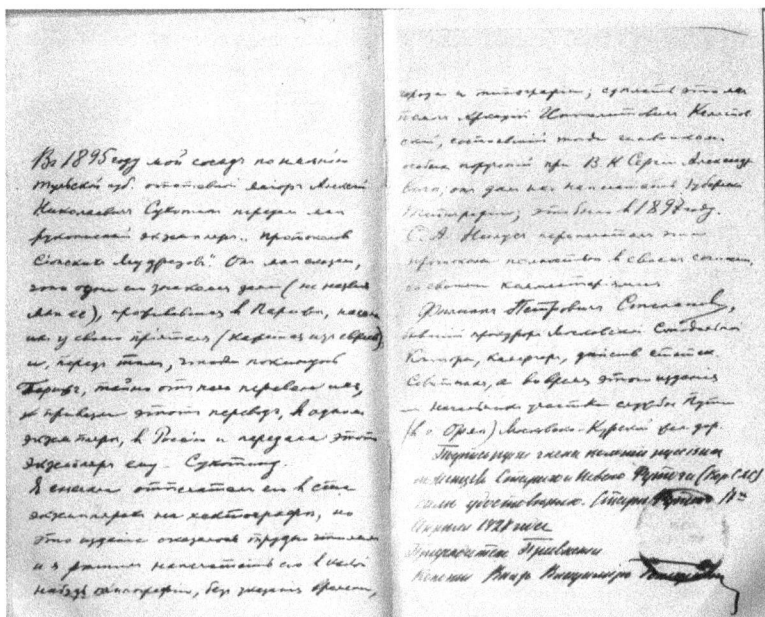

Figure 3.1 Affidavit of Filipp Petrovich Stepanov, 17 April 1927. Illustration from L. Fry, *Waters Flowing Eastward* (Chatou: British American Press, 1934, following p. 88). The original of the affidavit is said to be in the archives of the Holy Trinity Monastery, Jordanville, NY.

Filipp Stepanov's statement is one of the most important documents on the genesis of *The Protocols of the Elders of Zion*. For the first time, precise details are given here about the allegedly earliest printings of that text, which until then is said to have existed only as a manuscript. Not only the time, type, and circumstances of the copying are mentioned, but also the persons involved. It is therefore not surprising that Stepanov's testimony has since been repeatedly cited and controversially discussed in both the apologetic and critical literature on the *Protocols* (Cohn 1996: 108–109; De Michelis 2004: 23–24; Begunov 1996: 77; Platonov 1999: 198).

Stepanov's statement was published in 1931 by Leslie Fry, an American antisemite who – at times supported by Henry Ford – conducted research on the *Protocols* and gathered testimonies to prove their authenticity (Hagemeister 2014; see also Chapter 4). She presented the results of her research, which she carried out mainly in circles of Russian émigrés, in the book *Waters Flowing Eastward*, which was first published in Paris in 1931. The work, of which a French edition was also published in the same year (*Le retour des flots vers l'Orient. Le Juif, notre maître*), was a great success and soon became a standard work for conspiracy believers and *Protocol* adepts in ever new editions.

Fry was apparently well informed. Thus, she not only reproduced the wording of Stepanov's statement, but also published a facsimile of his note (Fry 1934a: 88).[1] She identified the lady mentioned in it as Iustin'ia Glinka (1836–1918?), a landowner in Orël.[2] According to Fry, Glinka had acquired the *Protocols* in Paris in 1884 with the help of the Jew Joseph Schorst and brought them to Russia, where they then reached Filipp Stepanov and Sergei Nilus through the intermediary of Aleksei Sukhotin (Fry 1934a: 87–88). Théodore Joseph Schapira or Schapiro, who called himself Schorst, actually existed. Born in Galicia in 1858, he is said to have spied on Russian revolutionaries in Paris together with a number of other mostly Jewish agents on behalf of Glinka. Allegedly, Schorst/Schapira was a member of a lodge of the rite Misraïm. Later he is said to have fled to Egypt and been murdered there.[3]

Fry also knew about Sergei Nilus (1862–1929), the most prominent editor and commentator on the *Protocols*. In the mid-1920s she had travelled to the Soviet Union to contact Nilus and, if possible, get him out of the country. The trip, however, seems to have been less than successful. According to Fry after her return, she managed to reach Nilus with great difficulty, but he refused to talk to her (Cherikover 1934a: 3). Nevertheless, Fry had exclusive information in this case as well: She was the first to publish a photograph of Nilus and gave exact details about the last years of his life and the time and place of his death (Fry 1934a: 88).

Filipp Petrovich Stepanov (1857–1933), the author of the statement quoted at the beginning of this chapter, was undoubtedly one of the most competent witnesses as far as the origin of the *Protocols* was concerned. A former Chamberlain and State Councillor, Stepanov had administered the Moscow Synodal Office from 1906 to 1917; in 1905 he was one of the founders of the Society for the Active Struggle against the Revolution, and later he was a member of the far-right Union of the Russian People. In Russia he had maintained close contacts with those reactionary circles and persons who are repeatedly mentioned in connection with the *Protocols*. Filipp Stepanov was even related to Sergei Nilus and his wife Elena Aleksandrovna Ozerova (1854–1938).[4] His brother Mikhail Petrovich (1853–1917), aide-de-camp and close confidant of Grand Duke Sergei Aleksandrovich and his wife Elizaveta Fëdorovna, is said to have initiated the connection between Nilus and Ozerova. While Filipp Stepanov lived in Yugoslavia after the Revolution (he died in Belgrade in January 1933), his daughter, Marina Filippovna Shoppit (1887–1931), a doctor of art history, had remained in Moscow and was in close contact with the Nilus couple in the 1920s (Anon 1937; Anon 1969: 40).

The Aleksei Nikolaevich Sukhotin (1848–1903) mentioned by Stepanov, a retired major, Marshal of Nobility of Chern' district in the government of Tula from 1898 and vice-governor of Stavropol' in 1903, is also a central figure in the history of the *Protocols*.[5] In his 1917 edition of the *Protocols*, Nilus stated that he had received a manuscript from him in 1901 entitled *Protokoly sobranii Sionskikh mudretsov*. Sukhotin had received the manuscript from a landowner in the Chern' district who lived permanently abroad and had obtained the manuscript "in a most mysterious way (probably by theft)" (Nilus 1917: 86).[6]

Stepanov's statement and Nilus' account seem to confirm each other. If what Stepanov testifies is true, then the *Protocols* already existed in a Russian version in 1895. In that case, their creation cannot be linked to the First Zionist Congress of 1897 (or subsequent congresses). It is above all the Italian slavist Cesare G. De Michelis who vehemently disputes Stepanov's statements, since they contradict his thesis that the *Protocols* were written in Russian between April 1902 and August 1903 as a parody of Theodor Herzl's *Judenstaat* and with reference to the Fifth Zionist Congress in 1901 (De Michelis 2004: 47–49). If, according to De Michelis, the *Protocols* were already available in print in Russian before the turn of the century, it is incomprehensible why Nilus received them from Sukhotin as a manuscript in 1901 and another editor of the *Protocols*, Georgii Butmi, dated their "translation from French" to 9 December 1901 (De Michelis 2004: 25; Butmi 1907: v, 78).[7] Finally, according to De Michelis, the well-known journalist Mikhail Men'shikov (1859–1918), who was the first to mention the *Protocols* in April 1902, spoke of them as "a fairly thick manuscript" (*dovol'no tolstaia rukopis'*), one or more copies of which circulated in Saint Petersburg. He did not mention a printed edition, however, because, according to De Michelis' conclusion, it did not yet exist (De Michelis 2004: 25, 35).[8] The Jewish lawyer Genrikh Sliozberg (1863–1937) also states in his memoirs that the *Protocols*, before they first appeared in print, had already "passed from hand to hand" in 1899 (Sliozberg 1933: 290). No copy of Stepanov's 1897 anonymously printed edition of the *Protocols* has yet been found.[9] However, there have been repeated references to a publication of the text produced by hectographic or lithographic processes. Lev Tikhomirov, the ultra-Orthodox monarchist and editor of the conservative daily *Moskovskie vedomosti* (Moscow News), remarked in January 1911:

> This document [the *Protocols*; M.H.] has been known for a long time. It first appeared as a translation from French about ten years ago, initially only as a manuscript, then it was lithographically reproduced [*byl izdan litografski*], after which, if we are not mistaken, there were two printed editions.
>
> (Tikhomirov 1999a: 328)[10]

In fact, by this time more than half a dozen printed editions of the *Protocols* had appeared. But what was meant by the "lithographically reproduced" text? Was it the same one that Filipp Stepanov had witnessed?

Research for the Bern trial

The question of the earliest publications of the *Protocols* arose again at the famous Bern trial, which lasted from 1933 to 1937, including the revision proceedings (see Chapter 2). In June 1933, the Swiss Federation of Jewish Communities (SIG) and the Jewish Community of Bern filed criminal charges against the disseminators of the *Protocols*, members and sympathizers of the National Front. The formal charge was distribution of "indecent literature". However, the declared aim of the Jewish plaintiffs was to obtain a court decision that the *Protocols* were a forgery. They sought to prove the forgery through a complete, self-contained, and convincing story about the origin of the text.

As can be seen from the internal correspondence of the Bernese lawyers, the plaintiffs had early on settled on the version according to which the *Protocols* had been fabricated in Paris by order of the head of the foreign agency of the Okhrana, Pëtr Rachkovskii, towards the end of the 1890s. The main witness to this was the French Count Alexandre du Chayla. As early as 1921, he had claimed in several newspaper articles that Nilus had shown him the manuscript of the *Protocols* in 1909 at the Optina Pustyn' monastery and confessed to having obtained it from Rachkovskii through the intermediary of his former mistress. The manuscript, according to du Chayla, was written in poor French and with different handwritings. Although there was considerable doubt among the plaintiffs about du Chayla's integrity and the veracity of his account, they stuck to his version and sought to substantiate it with further witnesses and documents.

On behalf of the Bernese lawyers, the Russian historians Il'ia Cherikover, Sergei Svatikov, Boris Nikolaevskii, and Vladimir Burtsev, as well as the lawyer Genrikh Sliozberg, researched in Paris, especially among their compatriots living in emigration. In Amsterdam, Alfred Wiener, founder and director of the Jewish Central Information Office (JCIO), collected books, newspapers, and magazines and evaluated them. The plaintiffs also approached Soviet authorities with a request to provide them with relevant documents from the Tsarist era. As a result, the lawyer Aleksandr Tager conducted research in various archives in Moscow and Leningrad as well as in the Lenin Library in Moscow and regularly reported on the results.[11] Several times between June 1934 and January 1935, he sent photocopies of documents that appeared relevant to Bern,[12] where they were translated and made available to the court's independent expert, Carl Albert Loosli, as well as to the plaintiffs' expert, Arthur Baumgarten.[13] However, Tager's research, which was compensated by the American-Jewish aid organization Agro-Joint, brought only meagre results. At best, it was possible to discredit Rachkovskii as a person on the basis of the documents found and sent as copies. No evidence of the authorship of the *Protocols* was found.[14]

The defendants had initially done nothing to defend their position. Only shortly before the beginning of the second main trial at the end of October 1934 did they succeed in obtaining an expert witness. Ulrich Fleischhauer (1876–1960), founder and head of the private antisemitic propaganda and news agency *Welt-Dienst* in Erfurt, agreed to provide proof of the authenticity of the *Protocols* in the further course of the proceedings.[15] Now Fleischhauer also started intensive research activities – albeit with a one-year delay. He also used his international connections to establish contacts, locate witnesses and obtain evidence. He found support among right-wing Russian émigrés. His most important collaborator, however, was the Austrian "professional antisemite" Hans Jonak von Freyenwald (1878–1953).[16]

In May 1935, the verdict was handed down. Judge Walter Meyer ruled that the *Protocols* were a forgery and plagiarism, and thus fell under the Bernese law against indecent literature. Two of the accused disseminators of the *Protocols* were sentenced to small fines but also to contribute to the high legal costs. The defendants' lawyer immediately applied for an appeal. The defenders of the *Protocols* hoped to be able to decide the case in their favour through new evidence.

In the course of 1936, Jonak von Freyenwald travelled to Poland, Yugoslavia, and France to collect material and question witnesses.[17] Near Posen, he met Sergei Sergeevich Nilus (1883–1941), the son of the editor of the *Protocols*, who worked as an estate manager. In a notarized statement, the latter affirmed that he had been a witness when Aleksei Sukhotin handed over the manuscript of the *Protocols* to his father on the Grachovka (Gouvt. Orël) estate in June 1901. Sukhotin had stated that he had received it from the widow of a nobleman who had found it in her husband's desk after his death. The manuscript was written in French, and his father then translated it into Russian in order to publish it (Nilus 1936).[18] In Belgrade, Jonak von Freyenwald met Count Illarion Lanskoi (1894–1984), who had many contacts with right-wing and antisemitic circles of Russian émigrés.[19] Lanskoi had known Filipp Stepanov and was friends with Prince Vladimir Golitsyn (1887–1974), who had authenticated Stepanov's 1927 statement. On 13 November 1934, Vladimir Golitsyn had made a statement to Lanskoi in which he essentially confirmed (albeit with variations) what Stepanov had stated to him in 1927.[20]

According to Golitsyn, Aleksei Sukhotin received the *Protocols* as a manuscript in 1897 from a lady whose name he did not want to mention. The manuscript consisted of several individual sheets and allegedly came from abroad. According to the style, it was a translation. In order to distribute it, Sukhotin gave the manuscript to his friend Stepanov, who, with the help of his friend Arkadii Kelepovskii, printed several hundred copies of it "as a manuscript" (*na pravakh rukopisi*) between 1897 and 1898 in the printing house of the Moscow Governor General. Stepanov had kept the original manuscript as well as the edition of the pamphlet in his flat; he had given a copy to Nilus, who had revised the text and published it in his book *Velikoe v malom* (The Great in the Small) in 1905. Contrary to Stepanov's statement, the Russian manuscript of the *Protocols* would have reached Sukhotin only in 1897. There was also no longer any mention of duplication "with a hectograph". Instead, we learn that between 1897 and 1898 an edition of several hundred copies was printed in Moscow, one of which Stepanov passed on to Nilus.

Jonak von Freyenwald also sought out Prince Golitsyn, but all he learned from him was that the pamphlet printed by Stepanov had had an edition of 200 copies and a pale blue cover. Jonak noted with regret that he had not been able to find a single copy of either the hectographed prints or the printed brochure.[21] From Golitsyn's wife Vera Filippovna (1885–1954), the daughter of Filipp Stepanov (and childhood sweetheart of Sergei Sergeevich Nilus), Jonak received a letter in which she repeated verbatim – this time in French – what her husband had declared to Lanskoi on 13 November 1934.[22] Vera Filippovna had already written the same to Nikolai Zhevakhov, another follower of the *Protocols*, who reported on it in his book on Nilus. Here, of course, it was said that Stepanov had not given Nilus the pamphlet he had printed, but the Russian manuscript of the *Protocols* obtained from Sukhotin (Zhevakhov 1936: 24).[23]

Through the mediation of Lanskoi, Jonak finally reached a cousin of Aleksei Sukhotin, Antoniia Porfir'evna Man'kovskaia,[24] who lived as the widow of Admiral Nikolai Stepanovich Man'kovskii in the Serbian spa town of Vranjačka Banja. There she stated to him on 13 December 1936:

About the year 1895 I visited my cousin A[leksei] N[ikolaevich] Sukhotin on his estate Medwegje [Medvezhki] (Chern' railway station) and saw the manuscript of the *Protocols* being copied by his sister Vera Nikolaevna Sukhotina and by Mrs Olga Feodorova Lotina, née Vishnevtzky [Vishnevetskaia], who is my niece. Vera died in 1920, Mrs Lotina now lives in Paris, as does her son Vasilii. I also know that Filipp Stepanov printed the *Protocols*. We often spoke of this in Russia.[25]

Since Vera Sukhotina had already died in Rostov in 1920, Jonak von Freyenwald set out to find Ol'ga Lotina, only to soon learn that she had meanwhile "lapsed into mental derangement", was living in an asylum for the mentally ill in Paris, and was thus "no longer fit to be questioned".[26]

However, there was the statement of two witnesses who said they remembered Lotina's earlier statements about the origin of the *Protocols*. According to these, a close relative of hers, apparently her cousin, together with another agent of the political police, had in 1897 drugged a participant in the First Zionist Congress, probably Nahum Sokolov, on his return journey, stolen from him the minutes he had brought with him and secretly transcribed them in stenographic form.[27] Further research by Lanskoi revealed that Lotina's "close relative" could have been Vera Nikolaevna Sukhotina. She lived with her brother Aleksei Nikolaevich on the Medvezhki estate in the government of Tula, a well-known meeting place for reactionary politicians and officials. Born in 1854, Sukhotina was 43 years old at the time of the First Zionist Congress. She was described as an ardent patriot, politically interested and eccentric in character, which is why, according to Lanskoi, she could have been trusted with a secret service operation.[28]

Let us note: Three witnesses (Stepanov, Golitsyn, Man'kovskaia), who are related to each other, agree that in 1895 (or 1897) a Russian manuscript of the *Protocols*, which was obviously a translation, was in the possession of Aleksei Sukhotin. According to the further concurring explanations, Filipp Stepanov had a printed edition made of this manuscript in 1897 or 1898. Only when it comes to the question of who passed the *Protocols* on to Nilus and in which version do the statements differ: sometimes Sukhotin is mentioned (Nilus and his son), sometimes Stepanov (Golitsyn, Golitsyna);[29] sometimes there is talk of a manuscript (Nilus and his son, Golitsyna according to Zhevakhov), sometimes of Stepanov's printed brochure (Golitsyn, Golitsyna). It is also conceivable that Nilus received both a manuscript from Sukhotin and a printed edition of the *Protocols* from Stepanov. In any case, he seems to have been in possession of the text by 1901 at the latest.

The version according to which a Russian translation of the French text of the *Protocols* already existed around the mid-1890s was also confirmed by a witness who seemed to be independent. On 9 December 1934, Gleb Verkhovskii (1888–1935), a Catholic clergyman of the Byzantine rite living in Chicago, addressed the American Jewish Committee with an affidavit.[30] Verkhovskii stated that in the 1890s, at his father's home in Saint Petersburg, he had met the members of a group that fought Sergei Witte's financial policy. The leader was the Slavophile publicist Sergei Sharapov (1855–1911); in addition to his father, the architect Evgenii Verkhovskii, the members included the economists Pavel Ol' (1874–?) and Afanasii Vasil'ev (1851–1929), the writer and Jewish apostate Savelii Litvin (Ėfron, 1849–1925), and the aforementioned Georgii Butmi de Katsman. According to Verkhovskii, the latter had travelled to Paris in 1895, shortly after the trial of Alfred Dreyfus, to establish contacts with French antisemites. On his return in the same year, he brought back a French manuscript, which he said was the *Protocols*.[31] Together with his wife Nadezhda Vasil'evna and Verkhovskii's mother, Mariia Karlovna, née von Stark, Butmi translated the manuscript into Russian.[32] This translation was published around 1896. Verkhovskii's statements, which he repeated on 8 January 1935 to Sigmund Livingston, the founder and first president of the Anti-Defamation League (ADL), also attracted the attention of the press (Livingston 1944: 40–41; Anon, 1935a, 1935b). However, they contradicted the version presented at the Bern trial by the plaintiffs and were therefore not considered by them; they soon fell into oblivion.[33]

The Litvin-Ėfron mentioned by Verkhovskii is cited as another informant who claimed to have known the *Protocols* before their first publication (Begunov 1996: 62). As Sheel' Khaimovich Ėfron, he had graduated from the rabbinical college in Vilna in 1870 and had subsequently converted to Christianity. Under the pseudonym Savelii Litvin, he wrote anti-Jewish stories (including about the uncovering of a Jewish world conspiracy) and plays (Dudakov 1993: 134–140; Reitblat 1994; Hagemeister 2017: 525). In 1920 he fled to Serbia and, through the mediation of his old acquaintance Mihailo Urošević, Bishop of Šabac-Valjevo, found accommodation in the monastery of St. Petka-Paraskeva, where he died in June 1925. Like other Jewish denunciators and apostates, Èfron also claimed to know closely guarded "secrets of Judaism", which he, however, only wanted to reveal orally to high-ranking officials or church people.[34] According to an unnamed witness, Èfron had known the "essential content" of the *Protocols* long before their first publication. This statement was quoted as the "confession of a rabbi" by Fleischhauer in his expert testimony (Fleischhauer 1935: 410–413). Subsequently, Jonak von Freyenwald collected further "witness reports" according to which Èfron had known the "true" origin of the *Protocols* from Jewish circles but had not told anyone.[35]

The copy of the Lenin Library

Back to the Bern trial. Among the documents sent by Tager to Bern were photocopies of a handwritten copy of the *Protocols*, which, according to the attached information, had been made "with a duplicating apparatus" (*na mnozhitel'nom apparate*) and was in the possession of the Lenin Library in Moscow. The copies were not published. Only a small circle of lawyers and experts had access to the material. Among them was Boris Nikolaevskii, to whom we owe the only description of this edition of the *Protocols* (Nikolaevsky s.d.):[36]

> In the collection of rare books of the Moscow Public Lenin Library … there is still preserved an edition of the *Protocols* which, to all appearances, is even older. This edition was reproduced lithographically and bears the title "Ancient and Contemporary Protocols of the Assemblies of the Elders of Zion", i. e. the same title as the subtitle on the pamphlet "The Root of Our Evils".[37] The pamphlet [in the Lenin Library; M.H.] does not contain any information about the time and place of publication, nor about the publishers. The *Protocols* are printed without any preface, commentary or epilogue. Particularly noteworthy is the inscription on the cover in Old Slavonic ornamental script, which is known to be used when printing and copying ecclesiastical books. The text is copied by hand, in two or three different handwritings. The book came to the Moscow library from a private collection that had been confiscated in the years of the Revolution, namely from the Pashukanis collection.[38]

Nikolaevskii then compares the text with the two earliest printed editions of the *Protocols*, the publications by Pavel Krushevan in the newspaper *Znamia* in August/September 1903 and by Sergei Nilus in December 1905.[39]

Unfortunately, we do not have the entire text of this edition of the *Protocols*. But even those individual pages that we do have clearly show that we are dealing with a third text that differs from the two mentioned above, and that this third text is the earliest: everything that is found in this text is also found in the other two, albeit with significant stylistic changes; on the other hand, those additions that distinguish the texts by Nilus and Krushevan are not present in the newly discovered text. In terms of style, this text is closer to the text by Nilus, who in turn based his publication on the newly discovered third text, but not only improved it stylistically, but also made some additions. Krushevan's text, on the other hand, differs more clearly in style from the lithographed edition. Even if one cannot say that this text [by Krushevan; M.H.] is a new translation of the *Protocols*, it is in any case a completely new adaptation of the translation; likewise, the additions in Krushevan's text are even more significant than in Nilus' text. ... with full conviction one can regard the newly discovered edition ... as the earliest of all those known to us.

(Nikolaevskii s.d.)

Although the plaintiffs' lawyers in Bern and their experts did their utmost to keep the Russian archival documents secret,[40] Jonak von Freyenwald had come into possession of the photocopies of the lithographically reproduced edition of the *Protocols* towards the end of 1936 through the defendants' lawyer Hans Ruef.[41] In order to find out whether it was the version produced by Filipp Stepanov, he had the photos presented to Vera Golitsyna. She, however, could not remember having seen that edition and denied that her father had been involved.[42]

Now Jonak von Freyenwald turned to the Austrian National Library in Vienna with the request to borrow the original mimeographed edition from the Lenin Library or to obtain photocopies; he also asked for information about the provenance of the work. The answer came immediately: In a letter dated 16 March 1937, the Lenin Library informed the National Library that the edition in question was not available and therefore no further information could be given.[43] Lawyer Ruef took this as an opportunity to cast general doubt on the authenticity of the Russian documents cited by the plaintiffs in his applications to the Revision Chamber.

The next to seek the mimeographed edition was the English historian Norman Cohn. Around the mid-1960s he was working on his book on the history of the *Protocols*, which was to become a standard work for a long time under the title *Warrant for Genocide*. Through his wife Vera (Brojdo), Cohn corresponded with Nikolaevskii, who gave him a great deal of advice and information. Nikolaevskii had long been convinced "that Rachkovskii had nothing to do with the writing of the 'Protocols' and could not have had anything to do with it at any point in his career".[44] He strongly advised Cohn to abandon the Rachkovskii thesis, as it stood in the way of further research into the *Protocols* (see Chapter 2).

Nikolaevskii also pointed Cohn to the Russian archival records at the Bern trial, of which the photocopies of the lithographed edition as what he believed to be the first text version of the *Protocols* had been "most valuable".[45] This edition, he informed him, had been produced by Filipp Stepanov in 1895 and was in the Pashukanis collection of the Lenin Library.[46] Nikolaevskii hoped to find the copies in his materials, but after Cohn repeatedly asked him for them, he finally had to admit that they had apparently gone astray.[47] Cohn then turned to the Lenin Library and was told in January 1966 that the edition he was looking for did not exist and had "never been included in the inventories".[48] At least, according to Cohn, the Wiener Library had a German translation of the copies sent to Bern (Cohn 1996: 109). But this too seems to have been lost there in the meantime, as De Michelis learned in 1996 in response to his enquiries in London and Tel Aviv (1998: 187).[49]

Five photocopied pages

In fact, five photocopies of the mimeographed handwritten edition have survived. Together with the other copies of the documents sent to Bern in 1934 and 1935, they are in the archive of the Swiss Federation of Jewish Communities, now held in the Archive of Contemporary History (*Archiv für Zeitgeschichte*) in Zurich (Hagemeister 2017: 93–94). The copies show the title page and four pages (1, 5, 22r, 22v) of the handwritten edition (of which the title page, page 1 and page 22r are shown in Figures 3.2–3.4). Attached to the photocopies is a brief description, dated 17 June 1934, sealed and signed by the Deputy Director of the Lenin Library Evgenii Rudnev (1881–1956). His signature, in turn, is elaborately authenticated by Soviet, French, and Swiss diplomatic authorities (Figure 3.5).

The precise comparison with other editions, which is now possible for the first time, shows that the text of the mimeographed handwritten edition is, as far as is known, identical to that of an anonymous, extensively annotated edition that appeared in print in Moscow in 1905: *Drevnie i sovremennye protokoly Sobranii "Sionskikh Mudretsov"*, Moskva: tippo-litografiia [sic] I.I. Pashkova, Miliutinskii per., d. Arbatskoi, 1905. 86 pp.[50]

The Zurich Archive of Contemporary History also contains the correspondence between Tager, the Bernese lawyer Boris Lifschitz and the "independent" expert Loosli.[51] In his letter of 19 June 1934 to Loosli, Tager reports a find that proves Rachkovskii's involvement in the production of the *Protocols*:

In the rare books section of the Lenin Public Library in Moscow, a manuscript entitled "Ancient and Contemporary *Protocols* of the Assembly [sic] of the Elders of Zion" was discovered, which had been reproduced with a duplicator, probably using wax paper. Neither the author nor the year of publication are recorded on the manuscript. The manuscript came to the Lenin Library in 1919 from the library of Vikentii Vikent'evich Pashukanis. It is clear from the notes in the Lenin Library that, firstly, this manuscript belongs to a much earlier period than the publication of Nilus' book and, secondly, that this manuscript was produced with the collaboration of Rachkovskii in the Police Department. Further extensive and in-depth archival research could bring to light documentary evidence for this statement. ...

The manuscript does not contain any author's notes and was apparently originally distributed without an indication of the author. The manuscript is written in two different handwritings. I suggest that you make enquiries to trace the persons to whom these handwritings might belong. In order to give you an idea of the manuscript, you will be provided with photocopies of the cover and of the first and last two pages of the manuscript. In this way you will also receive both handwritings in which the manuscript was written.[52]

This information caused a great stir among the Bernese lawyers, as it seemed that they finally had material proof of Rachkovskii's involvement in the fabrication of the *Protocols*. "We are impatiently awaiting", Lifschitz wrote to Tager on 13 July 1934, "the copy of the notes which are attached to this brochure in the library and from which it is clear that Rachkovskii had a hand in its creation".[53] Apparently Tager did not comply with this request. In any case, there is no further mention of the "notes" referring to Rachkovskii in further correspondence. Neither are their traces found in the archives, nor were they ever quoted. Nor is this important reference mentioned in a single word in the expert opinions of the plaintiff's side.

However, the alleged library records or notes have found their way into the literature. In his book *L'Apocalypse de notre temps*, published in 1939 and soon to become a standard work, the French journalist and secret service officer Henri Rollin claimed:

Finally, in 1934, the multiplying apparatus [!] and the manuscript used to publish the first known edition of the *Protocols* were discovered in Moscow in the former library of Mr. V.V. Pashukanis. A note on this apparatus indicated that this publication had been made with the participation of Rachkovskii.[54]

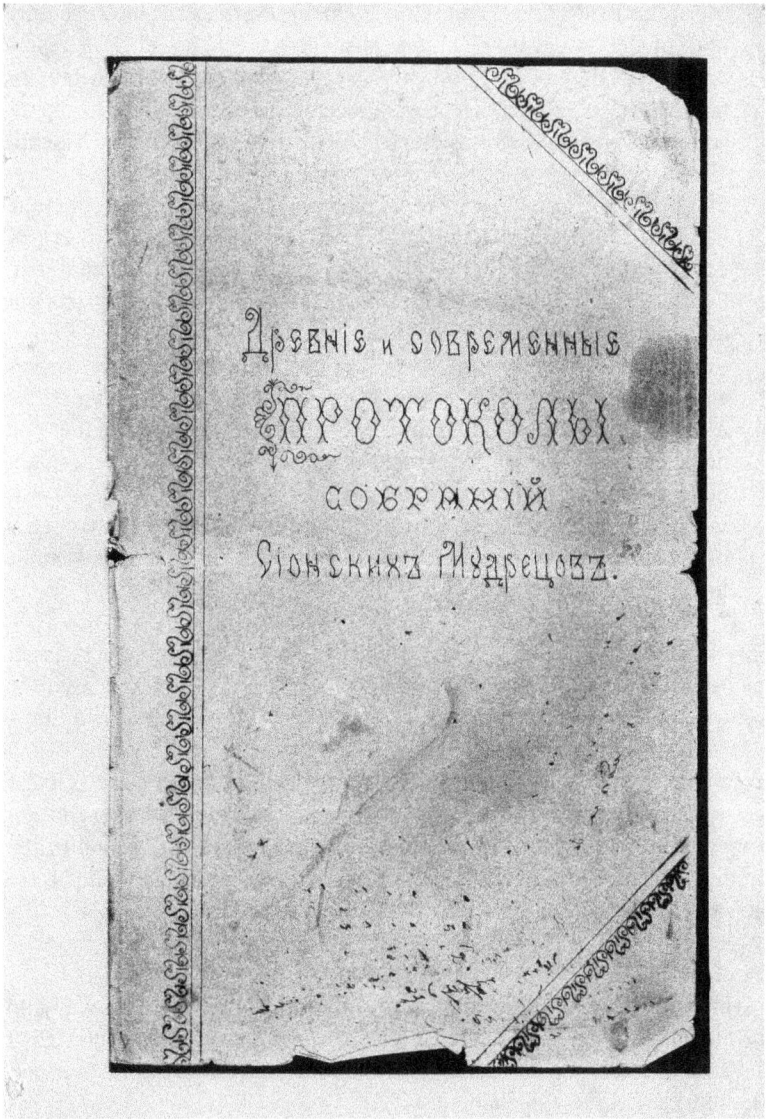

Figure 3.2 Title page of the handwritten copy of the *Protocols* in the Lenin Library, Moscow. (Photocopy, courtesy of Archiv für Zeitgeschichte, Zurich.)

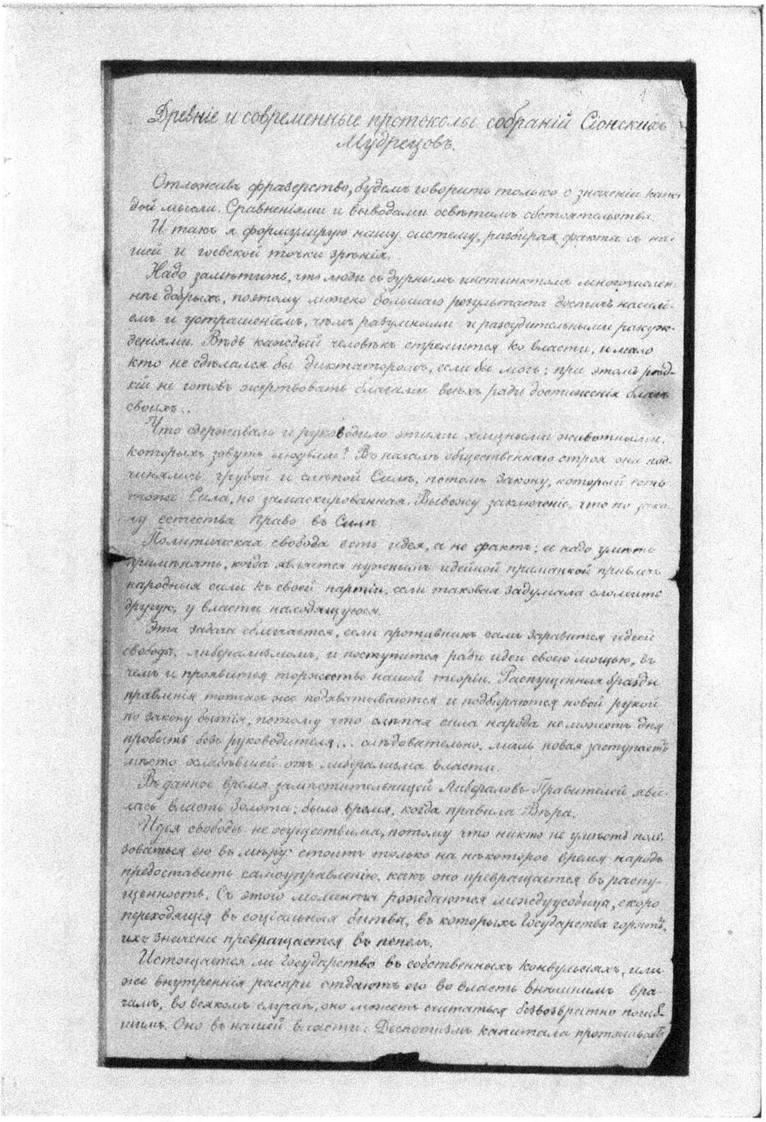

Древніе и современные протоколы собраній Сіонскихъ Мудрецовъ.

Отменивъ фразерство, будемъ говорить только о значеніи каждой мысли. Сравненіями и выводами освѣтимъ обстоятельства.

И такъ я формулирую нашу систему, разбирая факты съ нашей и гоевской точки зрѣнія.

Figure 3.3 Page 1 of the handwritten copy of the *Protocols* in the Lenin Library, Moscow. (Photocopy, courtesy of Archiv für Zeitgeschichte, Zurich.)

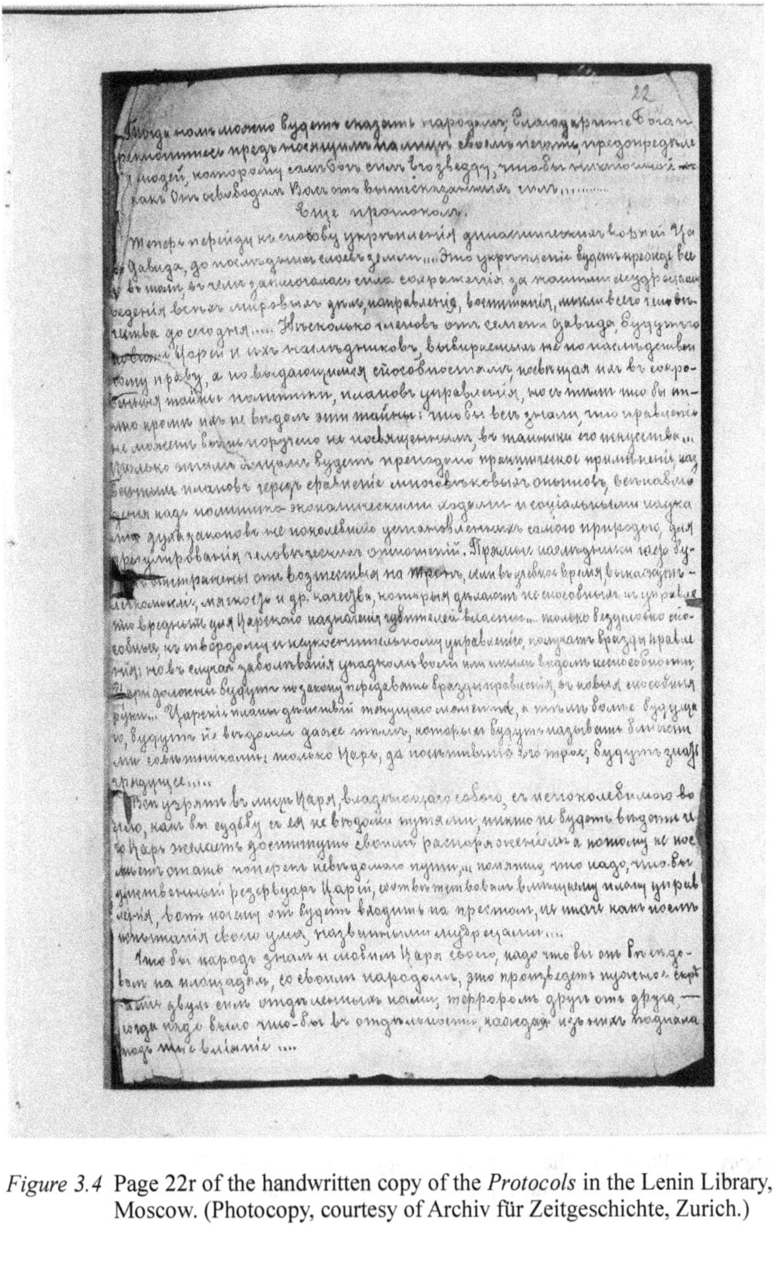

Figure 3.4 Page 22r of the handwritten copy of the *Protocols* in the Lenin Library, Moscow. (Photocopy, courtesy of Archiv für Zeitgeschichte, Zurich.)

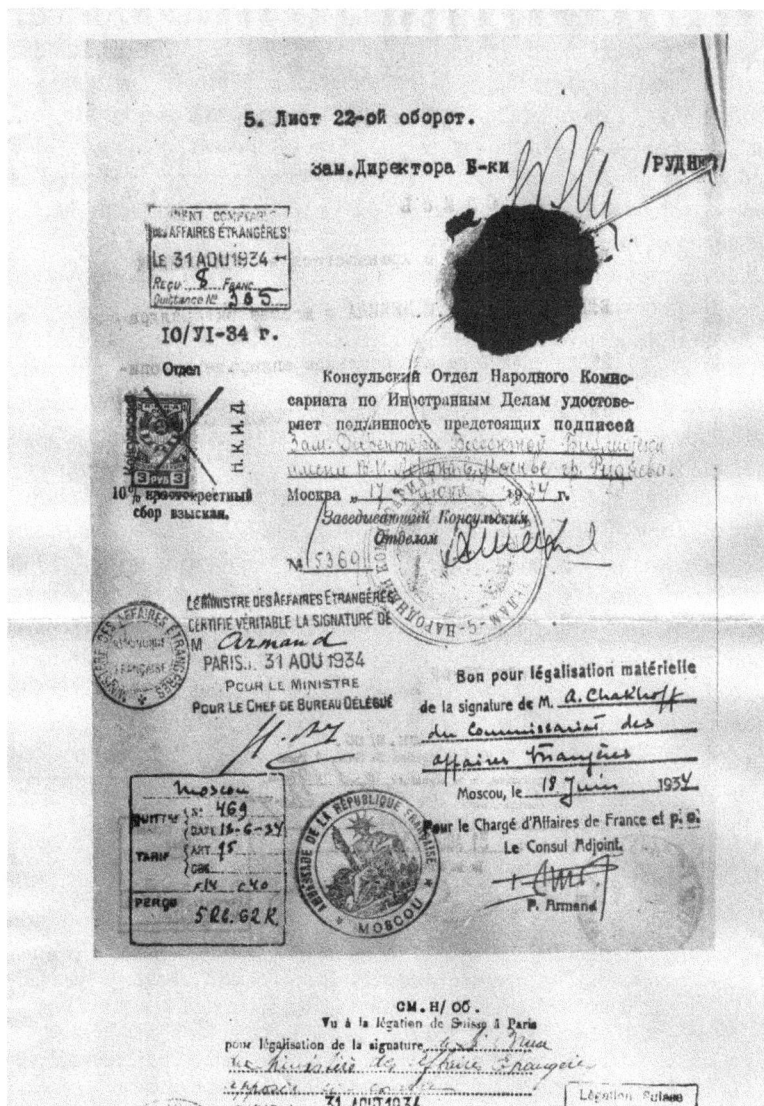

Figure 3.5 Certification of the photocopies of the *Protocols* in the Lenin Library, Moscow, sent to Bern. (Photocopy, courtesy of Archiv für Zeitgeschichte, Zurich.)

After the Bern lawyers had received the five copied pages of the handwritten edition, they endeavoured to obtain the entire work. On 8 October 1934, Tager wrote to Lifschitz: "I think that in the very near future I will be able to send you a complete photocopy of the lithographed edition of the 'Protocols of the Elders of Zion'".[55] On 3 January 1935, Tager wrote to Loosli to send him the "photocopies of the manuscript of the 'Protocols' produced with a duplicating machine, which is in the Lenin Public Library".[56] The copies were certified by the administration of the Lenin Library: "On each sheet is the stamp of the library". In accordance with Bern's request, it is now the complete copy of the edition mentioned. Whether the copies ever reached Bern is unknown; no trace of them has survived in the archives.[57]

Even if the copies of the handwritten edition lost in the Lenin Library do not offer a new textual variant, they are another piece of the mosaic in the early history of the *Protocols*, which is clouded by mystifications, speculations and lies. It is very likely that this edition is not identical with the one that Filipp Stepanov claims to have reproduced "with a hectograph" between 1895 and 1897, which means that its existence remains doubtful. Also, no copy of the edition allegedly printed in 1897 has been found so far. Thus, De Michelis' thesis that the *Protocols* were not written before 1902 remains unrefuted. On the other hand, several witnesses, including such credible ones as Sliozberg (1933) and Tikhomirov (1999a [1911]), have claimed that the *Protocols* were already in circulation in handwritten form at the turn of the century or even before. Could they (also) have been the lithographed edition of the Lenin Library? We do not know. What we do know is that this edition existed, at least until the time of the Bern trial, so it is not a mystification. The main question, however, remains open: Who wrote the *Protocols*, when, where and for what purpose?

Notes

1 Although the facsimile clearly shows the text of the declaration, it is often cited incorrectly: "Kellepovskii" becomes "Kamenovskii", and the printed edition is dated 1898 (Aronov 1991: 388). Charles Ruud (2009: xvi–xvii) dated Stepanov's statement to 1921 and claimed that it had never been published; he also asserted that a copy of the hectographed edition had reached Nilus already in 1897. Fry (1934a: 89) also made a mistake, misstating Golitsyn's first name as "Prince Dimitri Galitzin".

2 On the mysterious personality of Justina (Iustin'ia) Dmitrievna Glinka and her – still disputed – role in the writing and/or launching of the *Protocols*, see Aronov et al. (2006, 2011).

3 Information on his person in Morcos (1961: 495–496, 651) and in a letter from Andrei Rachkovskii to *Welt-Dienst*, 10 June 1936, Wiener Collection, University of Tel Aviv (WC): Bern Trial, box 16/16. One of the first editors of the *Protocols* had already claimed that they were "taken from the files of a

Masonic lodge of the Egyptian rite ... 'Misraïm'", a lodge into which mainly Jews entered (Butmi 1907: v–vi). A prominent member of a lodge following the Misraïm rite, which was considered anti-monarchical, secular and anti-clerical, was Adolphe Crémieux (Isaac Moïse, 1796–1880), first president of the *Alliance Israélite Universelle*, founded in 1860, which was repeatedly associated with the *Protocols* and the notion of a Judeo-Masonic world conspiracy.

4 Stepanov's sister Ekaterina Petrovna (1858–?) was married to Elena Ozerova's brother David Aleksandrovich (1856–1916).

5 On him and his relatives mentioned below, see Sukhotin (1908: 63).

6 In his first edition of the *Protocols* in 1905, Nilus had stated that he had received the manuscript in 1901 "from someone close to us who has since died". It came "from one of the most influential and deeply initiated leaders of Freemasonry ... in France"; a woman had stolen it from him (Nilus 1905: 321–322). The chapter that also contains the *Protocols* is entitled *Antikhrist, kak blizkaia politicheskaia vozmozhnost'. (Protokoly zasedanii sionskikh mudretsov). 1902–1903 gg.* Some authors – especially De Michelis – have understood the years as dating the *Protocols*, but they probably refer to the writing of the entire chapter, especially since Nilus states that he received the *Protocols* as early as 1901. In the 1911 edition, Nilus then calls the bearer by his first name, Aleksei (Nilus 1911: 52).

7 Georgii Vasil'evich Butmi de Katsman (1856–1919), from the Russian-based branch of a Dutch-Belgian noble family (Barons Boutmy de Katzmann) was a landowner in Bessarabia and one of the founders (1905) and chairmen of the "Union of the Russian People" (Hagemeister 2009b). In 1922, Butmi's version of the *Protocols* was published in Paris by the protonotary apostolic and conspiracist Mgr Ernest Jouin (1844–1932), as volume IV of the series *Le Péril Judéo-maçonnique* under the title *Les 'Protocols' de 1901 de G. Butmi*. Jouin, who was famous in Catholic circles at the time, used the 4th edition of the pamphlet from 1907, but mistakenly concluded from the date of the translation mentioned in the preface that the 1st edition had already been published in 1901.

8 De Michelis refers to Men'shikov (1902). First published in *Novoe vremia* 9372 (7/20 April 1902).

9 It is unclear whether the aforementioned government printing house was located in Tula or Moscow. In favour of the latter would be the involvement of Arkadii Kelepovskii (1870–1925), adjutant to the Moscow governor-general Grand Duke Sergei Aleksandrovich from 1892 to 1903 and later governor in Lublin, Lifland, Pskov and Khar'kov. In emigration, Kelepovskii was chairman of the Russian colony in Novi Sad and may have associated with Stepanov. His brother, Sergei Kelepovskii (1874–1928), nationalist deputy to the 2nd and 3rd State Duma, also lived in Novi Sad after the Revolution.

10 Lev Tikhomirov (1852–1923) belonged to the executive committee of the terrorist organization *Narodnaia volia* from 1879. From 1882 he lived in Paris, pursued by Rachkovskii and his agents. After his spectacular break with the revolutionary movement and the publication of his book *Pochemu ia perestal byt' revoliutsionerom* (1888), he was pardoned by the Tsar through Rachkovskii's mediation and returned to Russia, where he glorified monarchy and Orthodoxy in numerous publications. From 1909 to 1913, Tikhomirov was editor of the *Moskovskie vedomosti*. In 1914 he withdrew from public life in order to devote himself entirely to his religious-philosophical, esoteric and historical-metaphysical studies, which found expression in the work *Religiozno-filosofskie osnovy*

istorii, among others. Tikhomirov lived in Sergiev Posad from 1917. He had been acquainted with Sergei Nilus since 1903 at the latest.

11   Much of the correspondence is in AfZ: IB SIG Berner Prozess, box 174. Aleksandr Tager (1888–1939) had become known for his book on the Beilis Trial (1933 and 1934), which also appeared in English translation under the title *The Decay of Czarism*. The book was part of a planned trilogy, the other two volumes of which, on the Dreyfus affair and state antisemitism in Germany in the 1930s, never materialized. Tager was arrested in July 1938, accused of membership in a counter-revolutionary terrorist organization, sentenced to death on 14 April 1939 and shot immediately afterwards at the Kommunarka shooting ground. His research on behalf of the Bernese plaintiffs was honoured by the American-Jewish aid organization Agro-Joint. At the same time that Tager was conducting his research on the origin of the *Protocols* on behalf of the Bernese lawyers, the Leningrad religious scholar and ethnographer Mikhail Shakhnovich (1911–1992) was collecting materials on the history of the *Protocols* for an "anti-fascist exhibition", which was shown under the title "The Inquisition in the Past and Present" (*Inkvizitsiia v proshlom i nastoiashchem*) from October 1935 to July 1941 in the Leningrad Museum of the History of Religion (Atheism Museum). As Shakhnovich reports, there was a "small stand 'The Truth about the Elders of Zion'" at the exhibition (Mikhail Shakhnovich, Pravda o "Pravde o 'sionskikh mudretsakh'", unpublished typescript).

12   The Soviet side had strictly forbidden the Bernese lawyers to publish the documents and demanded the return of the copies after the trial was over. However, the demand was ignored.

13   Baumgarten, a legal scholar from Basel, acted as the official expert witness for the plaintiffs. The writer Loosli was only nominally the "independent expert of the court"; in reality he worked closely, albeit discreetly, with the plaintiffs' lawyers. This is clear from internal correspondence held in Archiv für Zeitgeschichte (AfZ), Zurich, and the Wiener Collection (WC), Tel Aviv (Hagemeister 2013, 2017).

14   The extensive file holdings of the Paris Okhrana were not in Russia, but in the USA. In the 1920s, they had been sold by Vasilii Maklakov, the Russian ambassador to France, to the Hoover Institution at Stanford University, where they remained locked away for 30 years. After they were opened, no references to the *Protocols* were found in them either (Fischer 1997; Blackstock 1966: 291).

15   On Fleischhauer and *Welt-Dienst* cf. Brechtken (1997: 43–61, 68–74); Schörle (2009, 2010).

16   Jonak von Freyenwald, of Bohemian nobility, was a lawyer and administrative official before devoting himself entirely to antisemitic agitation. From 1934 to 1941 he was a staff member of the *Welt-Dienst* and largely wrote the expert opinion for Fleischhauer at the Bern trial. Fleischhauer referred to him as "my chief snooper" and "passionate sleuth". Jonak von Freyenwald published his antisemitic writings under changing pseudonyms: "Dr. [Hans] Richter", "Dr. jur. Stephan Vász", "Karl Bergmeister", "Tibor Erdély". Most of his archive is now in the Wiener Collection, Tel Aviv. For his biography, see Hagemeister (2008b, 2017: 539–540).

17   Among the witnesses interviewed by Jonak von Freyenwald were the writer Ivan Rodionov (1866–1940), who had published the *Protocols* in mass circulation in Novocherkassk in 1918/19, and Andrei Rachkovskii (1886–1941), the son of the Paris Okhrana chief and owner of his father's archive (see Chapter 2).

18 On Sergei Sergeevich Nilus, see Hagemeister (2005a, 2017: 555). Jonak von Freyenwald maintained close correspondence with Nilus until his death and also sought to support him financially.

19 Nikolai Stepanov (1886–1981), Filipp Stepanov's son, had already established the contact at the end of 1934. Under the pseudonym "Svitkov", Stepanov agitated in emigration (first in Paris, later in Brussels) against Bolsheviks, Jews and Freemasons, also collaborating with *Welt-Dienst* in the 1930s. In his old age, he was ordained a monk in Hebron under the name "Alexander". His estate is in Holy Trinity Monastery, Jordanville, NY; materials on his biography in the archives of Vladimir Merzheevskii in Bakhmeteff Archive, Columbia University, New York.

20 A German translation of this statement is in WC: Bern Trial, box 18/24. A Russian version (original?) in the archives of Illarion Lanskoi at Holy Trinity Monastery, Jordanville, was not available to me. This is quoted in Platonov (1999: 199–200).

21 Note by Jonak von Freyenwald, undated (probably December 1936), WC: Bern trial, box 19/28.

22 Letter from Vera Golitsyna, Belgrade, 16 December 1936, in the archives of Jonak von Freyenwald, WC: Bern Trial, box 18/24. The only difference in content compared to the statement by Vladimir Golitsyn concerns the information on Arkadii Kelepovskii: while Golitsyn referred to him (erroneously) as the later governor of Ufa, it was now stated that he had been governor of Chernigov and Khar'kov.

23 Prince Nikolai Davidovich Zhevakhov (1875–1945) was personally acquainted with Nilus. Living in emigration in Italy, he was active as an antisemitic writer and publicist and maintained many contacts with like-minded people in numerous countries. In June 1944 he fled to Vienna to Jonak von Freyenwald and died there in April 1945 in an old people's asylum. On his biography De Michelis (1996, 2005), Hagemeister (2017: 584–585).

24 Man'kovskaia (1869–after 1938), was the daughter of Porfirii Nikolaevich Sukhotin (1821–?), an uncle of Aleksei Nikolaevich Sukhotin. See Sukhotin (1908: 65).

25 WC: Bern Trial, box 19/28. According to Jonak von Freyenwald, the statement was dictated to him by Man'kovskaia in German. Witnesses were Illarion Lanskoi and Prince Dmitrii Golitsyn (1914–1976), the son of Vladimir Golitsyn and grandson of Filipp Stepanov. See also Bergmeister (1937: 4–5). Cohn also refers to Man'kovskaia's statement and links this to the assumption that the two ladies had retranslated the Russian text of the *Protocols* into French (Cohn 1996: 110).

26 Note by Jonak von Freyenwald, undated (probably December 1936), WC: Bern Trial, box 19/28. Lotina's husband, Nikolai Vasil'evich Lotin (d. 1927), former State Councillor and Chamberlain, had first emigrated to Yugoslavia and lived from 1925 in Paris; their son Vasilii (1910–1962) became an architect in Paris.

27 Aleksandr Bartolomeichuk and Mikhail Shidlovskii, Svidetel'skoe pokazanie, Novyi Sad, 21 January 1935, typoscript, WC: Bern Trial, box 18/24. A similar version can already be found in the anonymous preface to the German edition of the *Protocols* by Gottfried zur Beek (i.e., Ludwig Müller von Hausen, 1851–1926) in 1920: Russian agents bribe the Jewish courier to bring the French "Reports of the Secret Meetings" from Basel to the "Judenloge" in Frankfurt and copy them in one night. In Russian, this version was distributed by Fëdor

Vinberg (1871–1927), who prefaced his edition of the *Protocols*; first in the antisemitic journal *Luch sveta* 3, Berlin 1920, then separately *Vsemirnyi tainyi zagovor*, Berlin 1922.

28 Illarion Lanskoi to *Welt-Dienst*, 16 February 1937, WC: Bern Trial, box 18/24; there also German translation of the letter by Nikolai Markov.

29 Nikolai Stepanov also asserted in a letter to *Welt-Dienst* that it was his father who had given the *Protocols* to Nilus (in which version is not stated). Nilus had only used the deceased Sukhotin as an excuse to protect Filipp Stepanov. Nilus' son then adopted this version. Stepanov to Detloff (i. e. Nikolai Markov), 15 June 1936, WC: Bern trial, box 17/21.

30 A copy of this statement in AfZ: IB SIG Berner Prozess, box 85. On Verkhovskii, see Iudin (2002).

31 "Returning to Russia soon, he [Butmi] brought with him a French manuscript to which he attached very great importance. This manuscript was the actual original of what is now known as the 'Protocols'". Differing from Verkhovskii's statement written in English, a Russian newspaper report published shortly afterwards states: "He [Butmi] brought with him to Saint Petersburg a manuscript in French – extracts from an old French work from which the compilers took dialogues for the fabrication of the 'Protocols of Zion'" (Anon. 1935a).

32 Butmi's wife pursued historical studies and published several antisemitic books (*Dogmat krovi*, Saint Petersburg 1914; *Kabbala, eresi i tainye obshchestva*, Saint Petersburg 1914; also in Czech, Prague 1925; *Tainye obshchestva i iudei*, Shanghai 1933). See Kartsov (1981: 114).

33 There is no evidence for the veracity of Verkhovskii's statements; the information about his parental home could not be verified either.

34 Numerous examples of such "Jewish informers" in Petrovsky-Shtern (2010: 56–62).

35 Statement of Vasilii Smirnov, 15 December 1936; statement of Vasilii Khoroshun, 3 February 1937, WC: Bern Trial, box 18/24.

36 There is also a German version: "Über die Entstehung der 'Protokolle der Weisen von Zion'. (Einführung)", typoscript, AfZ: IB SIG Berner Prozess, boxes 55 and 84. The Russian version is quoted below. Boris Nikolaevskii (1887–1966), historian and archivist of the Russian revolutionary movement, lived in Paris in the 1930s. During the Bern trial he coordinated the prosecution's testimony together with Cherikover. His extensive archive is in the Hoover Institution, Stanford.

37 What is meant is an edition of the *Protocols* entitled *Gde koren' sovremennoi neuriadnitsy v sotsial'nom stroe Evropy voobshche i Rossii v chastnosti. Vyderzhki iz drevnikh i sovremennykh protokolov Sionskikh mudretsov Vsemirnogo obshchestva Fran-Masonov*, which appeared in Saint Petersburg in December 1905. The cover is entitled *Koren' nashikh bedstvii*.

38 Vikentii Vikent'evich Pashukanis (1879–1920) was a connoisseur and collector of rare books and manuscripts on mysticism, spiritualism and Freemasonry. From 1917 he worked as scientific secretary at the Rumiantsev Museum. In December 1919 he was arrested as a "counter-revolutionary" and – despite the intervention of Lev Trotskii's wife Natal'ia Sedova – sentenced to death and shot in January 1920. Some of his confiscated books ended up in the rare books section of the Lenin Library.

39 Anon. (1903). "Protokoly sobranii Sionskikh mudretsov". in: Nilus (1905: 325– 394). Pavel (Pavolakii) Aleksandrovich Krushevan (1860–1909), antisemitic journalist, deputy to the 2nd State Duma, edited the newspaper *Znamia* in Saint

Petersburg from 1902 to 1905. On his biography, see Hagemeister (2008c), Zipperstein (2018).

40 Boris Nikolaevskii, however, had strongly criticized this. In a letter to Lifschitz, he complained that "the plaintiff party at the time – against the most elementary rules of any objective court procedure – had refused to submit the documents obtained from the Soviet archives to the defence for their perusal. This seemed to me even then to be completely incomprehensible and inadmissible". Nikolaevskii to Lifschitz, 10 August 1937, AfZ: IB SIG Berner Prozess, box 57.

41 Ruef had written to Tager about this on 19 August 1935, but received no reply. Letter in Staatsarchiv des Kantons Bern (StAB): BB 15.1.1557 e.

42 Bassowolo to Jonak von Freyenwald, 6 January 1937, WC: Bern Trial, box 18/24.

43 Jonak von Freyenwald to Ruef, 2 April 1937, AfZ: Nachlass Philippe Schwed, box 14.

44 Boris Nikolaevskii to Vera Cohn, 30 August 1964, The Boris I. Nicolaevsky Collection, Hoover Institution, Stanford (BNC): series 11, box 20, folder 24. Nikolaevskii attributed the authorship of the *Protocols* to the famous physiologist and reactionary publicist Il'ia Faddeevich Tsion (1842–1912).

45 Nikolaevskii to Vera Cohn, 15 August 1964, ibid.

46 Nikolaevskii to Vera Cohn, 30 August 1964, ibid. Nikolaevskii mistakenly dates Stepanov's 1927 statement to 1921.

47 Nikolaevskii to Vera Cohn, 25 November and 28 December 1964, ibid.

48 Vera Cohn to Nikolaevskii, 28 January 1966, ibid. An enquiry of mine at the Russian State Library (former Lenin Library) in 2008 led to the same negative result.

49 A copy of the German translation in AfZ: IB SIG Berner Prozess, box 55.

50 Available in the Russian State Library, Moscow: 116/52 (C); I 41/304. For a comparison of the texts, see De Michelis (2009). On the 1905 edition, see also De Michelis (2004: 10–11). Recently, a typewritten copy of the *Protocols* with handwritten corrections and additions by Georgii Butmi was found in the manuscript department of the Russian State Library in Moscow; it appears to be the earliest variant of the text and proves that the *Protocols* were composed in Russia (Ul'ianova 2021).

51 The correspondence with Tager was conducted in Loosli's name, but in fact it went through Lifschitz, who also made and certified the – often tendentiously falsified – translations from the Russian. Boris Lifschitz (1879–1967), a native of the Ukraine, had been a lawyer in Bern since 1909. During the Bern trial, Lifschitz, as chairman of the Jewish Lawyers' Commission, was significantly involved in the planning and execution of the trial. In March 1934, Lifschitz' friend Sergei Bagotskii (1879–1953), a representative of the Soviet Red Cross in Switzerland, had established contact with Tager. The latter, in turn, had been referred to Tager by Romain Rolland. Bagockii to Lifschitz, 26 March 1934, AfZ: IB SIG Berner Prozess, box 150.

52 Tager to Loosli, 19 June 1934, AfZ: IB SIG Berner Prozess, box 177.

53 Lifschitz to Tager, 13 July 1934, AfZ: IB SIG Berner Prozess, box 174.

54 "En 1934, enfin, on découvrait à Moscou, dans l'ancienne bibliothèque de M. V.V. Pachoukanis, l'appareil multiplicateur [!] et le manuscrit utilisés pour publier le premier tirage connu des *Protocoles*. Une note relative à cet appareil indiquait que cette publication avait été faite avec la participation de Ratchkovski" (Rollin 1939: 385). "Une note jointe à l'appareil utilisé pour ce tirage qui fut

trouvée dans la bibliothèque de V.V. Pachoukanis indique seulement qu'elle est antérieure à la première édition imprimée. Celle-ci parut en 1903" (ibid.: 33). As so often in his book, Rollin does not give a source for his claim here. Henri Rollin (1885–1955) was an officer in the French navy, a member of the secret service and editor and correspondent of the Paris daily *Le Temps* from 1920 to 1939. From 1941 to 1942 he headed the *Sûreté nationale* of the Vichy regime, although his part in the persecution or support of members of the Resistance is still disputed today. In February 1943, he allegedly went to London as an agent of the British secret service. Rollin undertook intensive research into the origin of the *Protocols* and in March 1935 attempted to purchase Rachkovskii's archive, which was in the possession of his son in Clamart. His book *L'Apocalypse de notre temps* went through eight editions in 1939.

55   Tager to Lifschitz, 8 October 1934, AfZ: IB SIG Berner Prozess, box 197.

56   Tager to Loosli, 3 January 1935, AfZ: IB SIG Berner Prozess, box 174. Loosli read this letter during the final hearing before the Bern court on 7 May 1935, but he did not refer to the complete copy of the handwritten edition either here or in his detailed opinion.

57   In a letter dated 16 April 1939, Nikolaevskii urgently requested Lifschitz, albeit apparently in vain, to send the complete photocopies of the manuscript edition, as it was of "enormous importance"; WC: Bern trial, box 29/38.

4 The American connection

Leslie Fry and *The Protocols of the Elders of Zion*

One of the most mysterious figures associated with the reception and dissemination of *The Protocols of the Elders of Zion* was the American Leslie Fry (1882–1970). Fry, whose origins and Russian connections are surrounded by legend, dedicated herself since the early 1920s to the fight against the alleged Jewish-Masonic world conspiracy. To this end, she spun a widely spread network to like-minded people all over the world. This chapter focuses on her research – apparently financed by Henry Ford – into the author of the *Protocols*, her efforts to propagate the text, and her clandestine support of the defendants at the Bern trial. It also attempts to shed light on hitherto unknown sides of her biography.

The origins of *The Protocols of the Elders of Zion* and the early story of their dissemination have provided a fertile ground for legends. If one turns *ad fontes*, as befits a historian, one cannot help but notice that they trickle only sparsely and that most of them are murky. Clues and traces have been covered and false trails laid, creating a labyrinth of half-truths and mystifications in which even serious researchers go astray. Only a few authors have tried to penetrate the thicket of history and fiction enveloping the *Protocols*; by far the majority have settled for repeating and elaborating upon the story which was formulated long ago by self-appointed witnesses. This is true not only of the apologists of the *Protocols*. The critics of this text have also greedily seized upon the stories which best served their interests without inquiring into their reliability.

Among the witnesses of the origins and the early history of the *Protocols* there are indeed more than a few figures of questionable repute, including a former Polish Princess who spent time in a prison in Cape Town for cheque fraud while claiming to be an eye witness to the fabrication of the *Protocols*,[1] or a French Count who as an antisemite had defended the blood libel traditionally directed at the Jews, but then in return for a generous payment stepped forward to become the crown witness for Jewish plaintiffs attempting to stop the spread of the *Protocols*.[2]

DOI: 10.4324/9781003200789-4

Things do not look any better when attention is turned to the camp of apologists defending the *Protocols*. Here we meet a Jewish apostate who claimed to know the secret plans for seizing world domination and who ended his days in an Orthodox monastery in Serbia,[3] or a Russian Prince and a protégé of Rasputin, who propagated the story of the *Protocols* from Italy and who at the end of World War II found refuge in a Viennese asylum for the elderly and the senile.[4] One of the most mysterious figures from the early history of the *Protocols* was, however, an American woman who, under the name of Leslie Fry, conducted not only extensive research into the origin of the text – whose authenticity as a document detailing a Jewish-Masonic conspiracy was for her beyond doubt – but who also did everything she could to spread the message of the *Protocols*, whilst she herself always remained in the background.

Family ties

Leslie Fry was very adept at hiding her origins and her life. In writings on the *Protocols*, she is mentioned only rarely, and those few references to her which can be found are contradictory. Historians Norman Cohn (1996: 77) and Il'ia Cherikover (1934b: 27), for instance, write that Fry was the maiden name of an American lady who was the wife of "a Russian" – Cherikover: "a Russian émigré" – called Shishmarev. Leo Ribuffo (1979–80: 447), on the other hand, believes her to be "a Russian émigré married to an American soldier". She herself consistently used the name "L. Fry" in her publications, but signed her correspondence with "P(aquita) de Shishmareff" (in Russian: "P.A. Shishmareva") or "Leslie Fry".[5]

Leslie Fry alias Paquita de Shishmareff was born out of wedlock as Louise A. Chandor on 16 February 1882 in Paris. She was the product of a lengthy affair between John Arthur Chandor (1850–1909) and Elizabeth Fry (née Red) Ralston (1837–1929).[6] Elizabeth's first husband had been the well-known Californian banker and bankrupt William Chapman Ralston (1826–1875), known as "the man who built San Francisco". John Arthur, the son of a certain Laslo Philip Chandor (László Fülöp Sándor, 1817–1894), an Austro-Hungarian immigrant to the United States who had been successful in Russia as an inventor and entrepreneur, had the reputation of being a notorious bigamist, "an adventurer of the most dangerous character" (Anon. 1877), an "inveterate liar" and "scoundrel in money matters" (Anon. 1889a); claims were also made that he was Jewish (Anon. 1889b: 505). A contemporary expose reported: "Chandor is a Russian Jew, and a naturalised American. His mother was a serf's daughter, and he is illegitimate; his father is an oil merchant, and has the lighting of part of Saint Petersburg" (Anon. ca. 1890: 42). In the 1870s and 1880s, John Arthur lived in Paris with his wife, Adeline Dickinson, and his mistress on the proceeds of his investments. Nothing reliable is known about Louise's youth. She is said to have studied at the Sorbonne and to have mastered several languages (Bondy 1946: 234). Apparently, she spent some time in Saint Petersburg while her grandfather and father were involved in business activities there. In 1906, according to author Guy Richards (1972: 196), Louise married Fёdor Ivanovich Shishmarev (1876–1917), a captain in the Russian Imperial Army, in Saint Petersburg. The Grand Duchess Kseniia Aleksandrovna and her husband, Grand Duke Aleksandr Mikhailovich, are reported to have acted as witnesses. The couple lived in Tsarskoe Selo, allegedly entertaining close relations with the court. The marriage produced two sons, Kirill (1907–1975) and Mikhail (1910–1983); Kirill's godmother is reported to have been the Grand Duchess Elizaveta Fёdorovna.[7] After the February Revolution in 1917 Louise Shishmareva fled with her sons and the family fortune via Tiflis and Vladivostok to San Francisco; her husband was said to have perished in the Civil War (Richards 1972: 61, 199; cf. Bondy 1946: 234).

Kirill Shishmarev attended the Mount Tamalpais Military Academy near San Francisco and then served in the French Foreign Legion from 1929 to 1934. Upon his return to California, he tried his hand as a technical director, writer, and film scenarist for Metro-Goldwyn-Mayer and Warner Brothers in Hollywood, but was boycotted by the film industry because of his mother's antisemitic activities. He distanced himself from his mother but, as documents prove, he himself had sympathies for the Nazis.[8] In 1939 he became an American citizen. During the Second World War, he served as an officer in the US Army (Chavchavadze 1990: 112–113). In the 1960s and early 1970s he lived in New York as Prince Kyrill de Vassilchikov-Shishmareff, Comte de Rohan-Chandor, where he was Lieutenant Grand Master in a self-styled Sovereign Order of St John of Jerusalem, Knights of Malta,[9] and endeavoured to track down the heirs to the Romanov inheritance. He claimed to be in contact with Tsarevich Aleksei, his former playmate in Tsarskoe Selo, who allegedly had survived the massacre in Ekaterinburg (Richards 1972: 61–66, 195–210).

Mikhail Shishmarev lived in London in the 1930s. In 1934, writing under the name Michael Fry, he published his impressions of a journey through Germany. His book *Hitler's Wonderland*, dedicated "à ma mère avec reconnaissance", sought to engender sympathy and understanding for the Nazi regime and the *Führer,* tempering this "with a certain amount of criticism". In a chapter entitled "This Jewish Question", Fry entered into a discussion about the *Protocols* as a likely source for Hitler's antisemitism, leaving aside, however, the question of the authenticity of this "amazingly prophetic" document (M. Fry 1934: 91–93).

Leslie Fry and the *Protocols*

It was after the Russian Revolution, at the latest, that Leslie Fry-Shishmareff became acquainted with the *Protocols*, whose ardent propagandist she was to become. It is possible that she came across them while staying in the Siberian area controlled by the forces of Admiral Kolchak, a notorious antisemite. In the summer of 1920, she sought out Henry Ford's personal secretary Ernest G. Liebold in Dearborn, Michigan, to draw his attention to the *Protocols*, at the same time recommending herself as thoroughly knowledgeable on Jewish machinations in Europe. She allegedly offered to sell Liebold the "originals" of the *Protocols* which were stored in a safety deposit box in a Shanghai bank – for $25,000 (Singerman 1981–82: 72; Ribuffo 1979–80: 447).[10] In September 1920 she was, according to her own account, employed by Henry Ford's Dearborn Publishing Company.[11]

In the 1920s and early 30s, Fry lived mostly in Paris and London. In Paris she kept the company of Urbain Gohier (i.e. Urbain Degoulet, 1862–1951), editor of the antisemitic journal *La Vieille France*, and of Monseigneur Ernest Jouin (1844–1932), the apostolic protonotary and warrior against the *Judéo-Maçonnerie*. Jouin had long maintained contact with Russian antisemites and had, in the early 1920s, published the *Protocols* in several volumes, copiously annotated.[12] Fry's further contacts included the publishers and propagandists of the *Protocols* in Germany, Ludwig Müller von Hausen (i.e. Louis Eduard Julius Müller, 1851–1926), Count Ernst zu Reventlow (1869–1943) and the Russian émigré and former colonel of the Imperial Guard, Fëdor Vinberg (1869–1927), who in 1920 published the Russian version of the *Protocols* for the first time outside of Russia.

In spring 1921, as the public discussion surrounding the *Protocols* raged, Fry published a sensational article in *La Vieille France* in which she claimed that the author of the *Protocols* was none other than Asher Gintsberg (Ahad Ha'am, 1856–1927), a proponent of cultural Zionism and a strong opponent of Theodor Herzl's political Zionism (Fry 1921b, 1921c, 1921d, 1923).[13] According to this account, Gintsberg had written down the *Protocols* in Hebrew[14] and, as leader of the secret society B'nai Moshe, had circulated them among the Jews of Odessa as early as the 1890s.[15] It was only later that the text was translated into French and reached the First Zionist Congress of 1897 via the *Alliance Israélite Universelle* in Paris. Theodor Herzl could not be considered as the author because he did not know Hebrew.[16]

In 1922, while in Scranton, Pennsylvania, Fry edited the antisemitic journal *The Gentile Tribune* (Jouin 1922: 199). At this time, she is supposed to have commissioned – apparently with financial support from Henry Ford – investigations into the origins of the *Protocols* and mustered witnesses to

prove the authenticity of the text (Jonak von Freyenwald 1939: 58–59).
The eminent Jewish historian Il'ia Cherikover (1881–1943) learned that
she travelled to the Soviet Union in the mid-1920s in order to meet the
most important publisher of the *Protocols*, Sergei Nilus (1862–1929), and,
if possible, to ferry him out of the country.[17] For this bold undertaking,
8000 dollars were allegedly placed at her disposal. Prior to her departure
Fry made contact in Paris and Berlin with relatives and adherents of Nilus
in the hope of obtaining information about his whereabouts and the circumstances under which he was living. With regard to the outcome of her
journey, Cherikover wrote (1934a: 3):

> Fry returned from her journey despondent and in a state of panic.
> Someone who spoke to her in Paris after her return from Russia,[18]
> claimed that she was even at that point completely distraught. She was
> shaking the whole time and she said that she had been recognized and
> almost arrested; she barely succeeded to save herself and leave the
> country. About her mission she only spoke in general terms. Nilus had
> refused to meet and speak to her, she only saw him from a distance, in
> a church. She did however succeed in speaking with someone close to
> Nilus whose words she took as if they were Nilus' own.
>
> This person stated that Nilus could give no information regarding
> the "Protocols" which he had once published, as he did not possess
> such information. It is not known whether Mrs Fry proposed to Nilus
> that he should emigrate. In any case, the relatives of Nilus living out-
> side Russia were resentful of the way in which she had pursued her
> goals by using money which had been foreseen as support for Nilus.

Fry had indeed succeeded in getting close to Nilus, who was living at that
time with his wife Elena Aleksandrovna (1854–1938), née Ozerova, and his
former mistress, Natal'ia Afanas'evna Volodimerova (1845–1932), in a sub-
urb of Chernigov, where they had been received into the house of a certain
Ol'ga Komarovskaia and her father, Mitrofan Komarovskii (Mikhailovskii
2000). Fry met there with Nilus' wife (Cherikover 1935b: 27). An acquaintance of hers stated in 1936 in an interrogation conducted by the security
service for the area of Chernigov that Elena Aleksandrovna had spoken in
1926 of a visit from an "American woman", who had brought along "shoes
or money",[19] Nilus himself also mentioned having once received a package
from Henry Ford (Orlova-Smirnova 1986: 63).

Fight against the "dark forces"

Fry put forth the results of her research, which seem to have been primarily conducted among Russian émigrés, in her 1931 book *Waters Flowing*

Eastward (the title is an allusion to Ezekiel, 47:1), which appeared through the same publishing house as Jouin's *Revue Internationale des Sociétés Secrètes* (RISS) in Paris (Fry 1931a). The book, which was translated into French later that same year (Fry 1931b), was a resounding success. It was reprinted numerous times[20] and soon became a standard work among conspiracy theorists and adepts of the *Protocols*. The book contains not only the complete text of the *Protocols* but also detailed comments on the history, organization, aims and methods of the alleged global Jewish-Zionist conspiracy and the influential people said to be behind it all.

It was here that Justine Glinka (1836–1918?) was first mentioned and the story told that she, with the help of a Jewish agent, Joseph Schorst alias Schapiro, had obtained the French manuscript of the *Protocols* in 1884 in Paris and taken it to Russia, where it eventually, via Aleksei Sukhotin (1848–1903), reached Filipp Stepanov (1857–1933) and Sergei Nilus.[21] Schorst, according to Fry a member of a Masonic lodge of the Mizraïm rite (which allegedly mainly attracted Jews), had sold the document to Glinka for the sum of 2,500 francs (Fry 1934a: 87–88; cf. De Michelis 2004: 118–120). After this he fled to Egypt and it was there that he was murdered.

Fry seems to have been well informed in this case as the mysterious "Schorst" did indeed exist. Born in Galicia in 1858 (according to other sources in Odessa in 1852 or 1854), his name first appeared on file as Théodore Joseph Schapiro (Schapira, Chapira, Zsapira), when he was commissioned in 1878 by the police president of Berlin, Guido von Madai, to spy on a social-democratic printing press. Sometime around 1880, he arrived in France, where he worked as a police informer under the name of "Schorst". Along with a number of other mainly Jewish operatives he was paid by Glinka for providing her with information on Russian revolutionaries. At the same time, he denounced her to her adversaries. Schorst-Schapiro had close contacts with members of both the left-wing terrorist organization *Narodnaia Volia* and leading anarchists, among them Pëtr Kropotkin and Lev Gartman. In 1882 in Nice he joined a British expeditionary corps on its way to the Sudan but soon after deserted in Egypt and secretly returned to France.[22] There are French police reports about him dating into the year 1896. Whether and to what degree he was involved in the "discovery" or the forging of the *Protocols* remains an open question.

Waters Flowing Eastward also includes the first reference to Filipp Stepanov's 1927 statement concerning the edition of the *Protocols* he claimed to have published in 1897; a document frequently cited later (Fry 1934a: 89; cf. De Michelis 2004: 23–26; Hagemeister 2012d: 161–164; see Chapter 3 in this volume). Stepanov made his statement for the antisemitic writer and *Protocols* "researcher" Aleksandr Nechvolodov (1864–1938), an émigré living in Paris. Finally, Fry published the first photo of Nilus, apparently acquired from his friends or relatives (Fry 1934a: opposite 85),[23] and for the first time provided precise information about the last years of his life and the date and place of his death (ibid.: 88).

In the course of her "research" on the global conspiracy of anti-Christian powers, Fry took aim at an ever-widening circle of adversaries. It was no longer only Jews, Freemasons and Communists, but also the Illuminati, Rosicrucians, Martinists, Mormons, Templars, Theosophists, Anthroposophists, Occultists, Spiritualists, Gnostics, Palladists and Satanists, whom she tracked with increasing fervour in order to uncover their dangerous schemes (Fry 1931c, 1934b). Her staunchest ally was undoubtedly Ernest Jouin, with whom she worked closely until his death in 1932 (Introvigne 1994b: 202–204, 232). Other prominent like-minded people included the antisemites and *conspirationnistes* Léon de Poncins (1897–1975), Henry Coston (1910–2001), and William Astor Chanler (1867–1934). In England, Fry was in contact with fascist and racist organizations, such as "The Britons" and its founder Henry Hamilton Beamish (1873–1948), and cultivated close relations with influential conspiracy theorists, such as Lady Queenborough (i.e. Edith Starr Miller, 1887–1933), the author of *Occult Theocrasy*, an encyclopedia of real and fictional secret societies, or Nesta H. Webster (1876–1960), the *grande dame* of modern conspiratorial thinking, who combined the delusional idea of a global conspiracy of Illuminati with premillennialist notions and thus met with great approval among ultra-right-wing Christian fundamentalists, most notably in the United States (Carlson 1943: 137; Introvigne 1994a: 46–47).[24]

In recognition of her services in the fight against the "dark forces", Fry was awarded the title of Honorary Dame (*Ehren-Ritterdame*) by the Imperial Constantinian Military Order of St George.[25] This order, which in 1924 received the blessings of Pope Pius XI, was a clandestine antisemitic and anti-Bolshevik organization founded in 1917 by Baron Igor Schmidt von der Launitz (1895–1976?), a rather mysterious character who self-styled himself as Prince Komnenos Palaeolog, Duke of Theodoro and all Gothia etc. Among the order's members were Nikolai Zhevakhov and the German right-wing occultist Rudolf von Sebottendorf (1875–1945) (Comnène Paléologue 1965: 7).

In the 1930s Fry worked for the German *Welt-Dienst* (World-Service), a private propaganda and news agency, founded in Erfurt in 1933 by Ulrich Fleischhauer (1876–1960), a retired colonel, and Georg de Pottere (1875–1951), a former Austro-Hungarian diplomat. *Welt-Dienst* was dedicated to "the resolution of the Jewish question" and the dissemination of the *Protocols*. Fry operated there under the aliases "Mme. Laurier", "Mme. Gordon", and "Mme. de Schischmareff". She was said to have been listed twice on the *Welt-Dienst* honour roll (Carlson 1943: 137; Bondy 1946: 149–150), but no further details about her "achievements" are known.

The famous Bern trial on the *Protocols* (1933–1935) did not include Fry – neither her theory of Gintsberg's authorship nor the "Glinka version" suited the argument of the *Protocols*'s defence (cf. Jonak von Freyenwald 1939: 96–97, 138–139; Hagemeister 2017: 107). Nevertheless, she corresponded from London and Paris with the anti-Jewish supporters of the defendants, Ubald von Roll (1908–1976), head (*Gauführer*) of the Bern district of the National Front, and Boris Tödtli (1901–1944), a Swiss fascist and antisemite born in Russia, both living in Bern, and Princess Mary Karadja (1868–1943), the eccentric founder of a Christian Aryan Protection League in Locarno, and offered them her help.[26] All the while she desired, as she wrote to von Roll, to remain hidden from view: "It is more than useless to mention me either as a witness or otherwise. Silence and discretion are more necessary than ever, and any indiscretion can only be harmful to us".[27]

In Paris, Fry discussed the trial with Nikolai Markov (1866–1945), leader of the extreme right in Tsarist Russia and since 1935 an associate of Fleischhauer in *Welt-Dienst*, and the former head of the Okhrana Aleksandr Spiridovich (1873–1952).[28] She also paid several visits to Andrei Rachkovskii (1886–1941), son of Pëtr Rachkovskii (1851–1910), the former head of the Okhrana's Foreign Agency in Paris and alleged forger of the *Protocols*, who was living in Clamart near Paris and had kept his father's extensive archive.[29] On the basis of the documents this archive contained, Fry wrote a long article "Occultism in Tsarist Russia. Philippe – Nilus – Rasputin", which she published in October 1935 in the first issue of her journal *Free Press*.[30] In March 1935 Fry made a sudden appearance at von Roll's in Bern, to strengthen the position of the *Protocols*-defence.[31]

On 13 April 1935, two weeks before the final court session, a report appeared in the Paris émigré newspaper *Poslednie novosti* (Latest News) about a "Princess Golitsyna" – found begging in Paris' 7th Arrondissement for money to pay for the treatment of her son, who was apparently in hospital in Bern. According to the paper, there was no son, and the apparent "princess" was actually Lidiia Shishmareva, née Svechina, a drug addict with a criminal conviction; widow of a captain in the Russian army (Anon. 1935c: 4). It seems that this was a bogus story; a satire of the way in which Leslie Fry-Shishmareva and her dedicated media work (the *Vieille France* was located in the 7th Arrondissement) was supposed to "save" the *Protocols* on trial at Bern.

In the mid-1930s Fry returned to the United States and settled in Santa Monica, California, using another house in nearby Glendale for an office address. This was her base in the following years as she created and coordinated a national network of propaganda and subversion and was soon considered the chief Fascist propagandist in Southern California (Lavine 1940: 196–200; Carlson 1943: 137; Bondy 1946: 149–150, 233–235).[32] Clearly now supported with abundant financial means – rumours suggested that some of the money came directly from Goebbels' Ministry of Public Enlightenment and Propaganda (Lavine 1940: 198) – she started a campaign against Jews and Communists in government and joined the opposition to Roosevelt's New Deal, which she called "Jew Deal", attributing it to the machinations of the Jewish Kahal to bring about an international financial system directly under its control. For this purpose, she founded the American Anti-Communist Federation, the American League of Christian Women, and the Militant Christian Patriots (which had a branch in England, also led briefly by Fry), and the monthly newspaper *Christian Free Press*.

From the late 1930s onward, "Mrs. Leslie Fry, alias Paquita Louise De Shishmareff" appears again and again as a "mysterious figure" in the reports of the House Committee on Un-American Activities and in the files of the Great Sedition Trials, but the evidence was never sufficient to secure a conviction. In 1939, in order to avoid arrest by the FBI, Fry fled to Germany (Carlson 1943: 139) or Italy (Jeansonne 1996: 229). Some of her

Figure 4.1 Leslie Fry and her allies. From left to right: Henry Douglas Allen, Conrad Chapman, Ivan Gurin, ca. 1937. (Courtesy of Special Collections and Archives, Oviatt Library, California State University, Northridge: Community Relations Committee Collection, pt. 2, box 254, folder 14.)

like-minded associates began to suspect her of being "an OGPU spy" who was working to disrupt the Fascist movement (Lavine 1940: 196).

After the attack on Pearl Harbour, Fry returned to the United States and was interned on Ellis Island for the duration of the war as "a dangerous alien" (Jeansonne 1996: 228). Back in Glendale after the War, she participated energetically in the subsequent persecution of the Communists. In the United Nations, she saw an embryonic world government with the aim of enslaving the gentiles under the banner of Zionism. A concerted effort, she claimed, was underway to create a universal Mosaic religion. This anti-Christian campaign would find expression in the secret tenets of Masonry, Illuminism, and Talmudic-Kabbalist Judaism (Fry 1958). Fry's network included racist organizations such as the Ku Klux Klan, as well as Christian fundamentalists and antisemites, such as the Catholic "radio priest" Charles Coughlin (1891–1979) and Denis Fahey (1883–1954), who emerged as advocates of the *Protocols*. On 15 July 1970, Paquita "Mady" de Shishmareff, alias Leslie Fry, died a quiet death in Fullerton, California,[33] but the poisonous seeds she sowed during her lifetime did spring up, and the effects of her work as a writer and activist continue to be felt even today.

Notes

1 Catherine Kolb-Danvin (1858–1941), former Princess Katarzyna Radziwiłłowa; cf. Aronov et al. (2009); Hagemeister (2012a). See Chapter 2 in this volume.
2 Alexandre du Chayla (1885–1947); cf. Hagemeister (2017: 520–521 and passim).
3 Sheel' Éfron-Litvin (1849–1925); cf. Hagemeister (2017: 525).
4 Nikolai Zhevakhov (1875–1945); cf. De Michelis (1996); Hagemeister (2017: 584–585 and passim).
5 Further names used are "Paquita Louise De Shishmareff", "Louise Fry" and – among her followers – "Mady" and "Auntie" (Carlson 1943: 137).
6 See,   https://de.findagrave.com/memorial/114297387/john-arthur-chandor; accessed 17 March 2021. There is no record of Louise's birth in the records of the *État civil* of Paris.
7 Richards' account of Louise's life and activities in Russia prior to the Revolution of 1917 is based exclusively on detailed information provided by her son Kirill. This information however could not be corroborated by any written documents. In any case, long-standing business connections cultivated by her grandfather may have paved Louise's way to Russia. She allegedly told a confidant that her two sons were born in Riga (Lavine 1940: 197). As for Fëdor Shishmarev, there is no evidence of his proximity to the court. His personnel file only shows that he belonged to the hereditary nobility of the government of Tver' and that he retired from military service in 1909 in Saint Petersburg with the rank of captain. He was not a graduate of the fashionable Corps des Pages in Saint Petersburg nor did she serve in a guard regiment. Fëdor Ivanovich Shishmarev, personal file, Russian State Military Archive (RGVA), Moscow: *fond* 409, *opis'* 1, *p/s* 263–984, *listy* 1–4; *opis'* 2, *delo* 3632, *listy* 12–13. For this reason, it is

far more likely that the entire story about the close relations with the court was fabricated by Kirill.

8 See the documents in Urban Archives Center, Oviatt Library, California State University, Northridge: Special Collections and Archives, Community Relations Committee Collection, pt. 2, box 62, folders 6–8, 10, 15–16; box 211 folders 5–8. Cf. fn. 32.

9 According to its website, the order's mission was the fight against the "International Conspiracy" of the Bolsheviks, Zionists and Socialists. Paquita de Shishmareff was linked to the order as a civilian expert on the so-called "Jewish Problem". The order boasted of its distribution of "anti-Bolshevik information" such as the *Protocols of the Elders of Zion*. http://www.spirituallysmart.com /History_After_Malta.html; accessed 20 April 2013. See also Coogan (1999: 603–606; 2021: 269–280).

10 This sort of proposal was no rarity at that time. A certain D. Rodionov, for instance, offered to sell the "Hebrew originals" of the *Protocols,* which were being stored with "a secret Russian anti-Jewish propaganda institution" near Harbin, Manchuria, to Ford's employees (Hapgood 1922: 48, 133), whereas Casimir Pilenas (alias Palmer), an agent of the Military Intelligence Division, tried to sell a copy of the *Protocols* for $50,000 to the American Jewish Committee (Szajkowski 1974: 157). As late as 2011, the Library of the University of Chicago acquired a hand-written copy of the *Protocols,* dated Shanghai, 1921, which had been advertised by a British antiquarian book dealer as a sensational offering at 5,000 pounds sterling.

11 See the affidavit by "Leslie Fry-Shishmareff", New York, 10 May 1923, published in English and in German translation in an anonymous article by Ernst zu Reventlow in his antisemitic paper *Reichswart* (Reventlow 1923: 3).

12 From 1921 Fry published regularly, albeit often anonymously, in Jouin's *Revue Internationale des Sociétés Secrètes.* One of her first publications was on the reception of the *Protocols* in the United States (Fry 1921a).

13 The Russian and German editions were collated by Fëdor Vinberg, who also wrote a preface and afterword. See also Flämming (1921).

14 In Vinberg's translation it becomes "Ancient Hebrew" (*drevne-evreiskii iazyk*). However, it would then have been impossible to reproduce all the modern terms in the *Protocols.* Only modern Ivrit created appropriate words for them.

15 In her affidavit of 10 May 1923, Fry declared that in 1920 "a Jew by the name of Bernstein, Editor of the *Free Press* in Detroit", had told the editors of the *Dearborn Independent* and Henry Ford's personal secretary that he "had known of the Protocols for a very long time, having read them in the Hebrew language in the city of Odessa, Russia, twenty years earlier" (Reventlow 1923: 3).

16 This argument has often been repeated and defended by devotees of the *Protocols,* for example Ludwig Müller von Hausen, publisher in 1920 of the first German edition of the *Protocols,* the like-minded Count Ernst zu Reventlow, and most recently the Russian historian and conspiracy theorist Oleg Platonov (1999: 364–382).

17 Here and hereinafter Cherikover (1934a: 2–3); cf. Cherikover (1934b: 27).

18 This was Nilus' niece Elena Kartsova (1893–1989), who lived at this time in Paris and who corresponded with Nilus and his wife. Kartsova's papers were acquired by the Hoover Institution, Stanford, in 2017.

19 Margarita Milovidova, interrogated by the NKVD, 14 August 1936 (Anon. 1994: 15–16).

20 Further revised editions appeared in 1933 und 1934 in France. Revised and expanded by Denis Fahey, *Waters Flowing Eastward*. *The War Against the Kingship of Christ* was published in 1953 and 1965 in London, and in 1988, 1997, 1999, and 2000 in the United States.

21 On Glinka, see Aronov et al. (2011).

22 Details about him are to be found in Paris, Archives de la Préfecture de Police: Dossier Théodore Schapiro (1879–1896), B^A 926. See also Morcos (1961: 495–496, 651), Hagemeister (2017: 567), and letter from Andrei Rachkovskii to *Welt-Dienst*, 10 July 1936; Tel Aviv, Wiener Collection: Bern Trial, box 16/16.

23 The undated photo was probably taken in 1927 or 1928 in Chernigov.

24 The plan "uncovered" by Webster, in which the Illuminati (composed of Freemasons and secular Jews) would destroy Christian culture, take over world domination and establish the "Reign of the Antichrist", bears many resemblances with the *Protocols* (cf. Ruotsila 2004: 114–115).

25 Igor von der Launitz to *Welt-Dienst*, 1 December 1934; Tel Aviv, Wiener Collection: Bern Trial, box 16/16.

26 Copies and photocopies of the correspondence, conducted in French, between Fry and Ubald von Roll (November–December 1934), Archiv für Zeitgeschichte (AfZ), Zurich: Nachlass Philippe Schwed; Tel Aviv, Wiener Collection (WC): Bern Trial, box 16/20 and 20. The same archives contain references to correspondence with Karadja. Further, a cryptic letter to Boris Tödtli signed "P.A. Shishmareva" in a simple, flawed Russian, WC: Bern Trial, box 24. Contact was established with the help of Fry's long-term ally Conrad Chapman (1896–1989), a wealthy Bostonian scholar.

27 "Il est plus qu'inutile de me mentionner soit comme témoin ou autrement. Le silence et la discrétion sont plus nécessaires que jamais, et toute indiscrétion ne peut que nous être nuisible". Leslie Fry to Ubald von Roll, 6 December 1934, AfZ: Nachlass Philippe Schwed, box 6; see Hagemeister (2017: 230).

28 Nikolai Markov to Boris Tödtli, 20 March 1935, WC: Bern Trial, box 21/30; see Hagemeister (2017: 268).

29 Leslie Fry to Ubald von Roll, 8 December 1934, WC: Bern Trial, box 20. Andrei Rachkovskii to Boris Tödtli, 17 August 1935, ibid., box 23; see Hagemeister (2017: 232, 312).

30 German translation made by Hans Jonak von Freyenwald, WC: Bern Trial, box 16/16.

31 Ubald von Roll to Mary Karadja, 1 March 1935, AfZ: IB SIG Berner Prozess, box 16; Hagemeister (2017: 262).

32 A wealth of materials for research into the antisemitic and Fascist network in California was compiled in the 1930s and early 1940s by members of the Jewish defence organization "Jewish Community Committee" (JCC; from 1941 "Community Relations Committee", CRC) in Los Angeles. Among them are extensive dossiers on Leslie Fry. Urban Archives Center, Oviatt Library, California State University, Northridge: Special Collections and Archives: Community Relations Committee Collection, pt. 2, box 21, folder 20; box 62, folders 6–16; box 211, folders 2–8; box 236, folder 16; box 251, folder 13; box 254, folder 14. In the latest book on Nazi activity in California, based on these materials, however, Fry's background is only touched on briefly (Ross 2017: 232).

33 https://de.findagrave.com/memorial/114297269/paquita-de-shishmareff; accessed 17 March 2021.

5 "The Antichrist as an imminent political possibility"

Sergei Nilus and the apocalyptical reading of *The Protocols of the Elders of Zion*

To this day, Sergei Nilus (1862–1928) is still considered the most prominent editor, commentator, and promotor of *The Protocols of the Elders of Zion*. After an outline of his biography, contrasting the numerous legends with established facts, Nilus' apocalyptic worldview, which determined his reading of the *Protocols* and his commentary on them, is presented in great detail. Nilus, it will be argued, interpreted the *Protocols* in a religious, eschatological context and believed to detect in them the secret plan according to which the powers of darkness, the Jewish Antichrist and his earthly allies, wage their war against Christianity.

Sergei Nilus, the most prominent editor, commentator, and promotor of *The Protocols of the Elders of Zion*, has become a kind of media star in the West. His image is that of an enigmatic and at the same time surprisingly versatile figure. In Will Eisner's graphic novel, *The Plot: The Secret Story of the Protocols of the Elders of Zion*, where the origins of the *Protocols* are presented as a conspiracy story – a conspiracy of cunning secret agents and sinister reactionaries – Nilus appears as a grey-haired mystic who is often invited to the Russian court, a competitor to Rasputin, a professor, and a fanatical antisemite (Eisner 2005).[1]

According to Umberto Eco, however, who wrote the introduction to Eisner's book, Nilus was not a professor but an "itinerant monk, ... half prophet and half scoundrel" (Eco 1994: 137; 1998: 17). Nilus "the monk" began his wanderings as early as 1988, namely in chapter 92 of Eco's novel *Foucault's Pendulum*, a book that can be seen as a fictionalized encyclopedia of occult teachings and conspiracy theories.[2] Eco was probably influenced by the Serbian author Danilo Kiš. In his story *The Book of Kings and Fools*, first published in 1983, Nilus appears as an "eccentric hermit", for insiders simply "father Sergius" (Kiš 1990: 136). Likewise, Nilus appears in books of which it is hard to tell whether they are based in fiction or fact, for example, in the occult conspiracy story *The Spear of Destiny* by Trevor Ravenscroft, in Hadassa Ben-Itto's (2005) semifictional story of the

DOI: 10.4324/9781003200789-5

1905
Russia
The First Publication

Figure 5.1 Sergei Nilus, caricatured. From *The Plot: The Secret Story of the Protocols of the Elders of Zion* by Will Eisner. Copyright © 2005 by Will Eisner Studios, Inc. Used by permission of W. W. Norton and Company, Inc. (New York, p. 61).

famous Bern trial on the *Protocols*, and in the international bestseller *The Holy Blood and the Holy Grail*. In the latter, Nilus is described as "a rather contemptible individual known to posterity under the pseudonym of Sergei Nilus" (Baigent et al. 1990: 198–199).

When we turn to the scholarly literature on the *Protocols*, the picture becomes even more confused: The enigmatic Nilus appears in various guises: not only as a professor or a monk but also as a priest of the Russian Orthodox Church, an Orientalist, a court nobleman, a journalist, a half-crazy pseudomystic, a zoologist, a mediocre lawyer, a religious philosopher, an agent of the secret police, an Orthodox theologian, and even a former play-boy. Some believe that Nilus was not his real name; some consider him the actual author of the *Protocols* (Hagemeister 2012c 143–150).[3] None of this is accurate.

Nilus the writer

Sergei Aleksandrovich Nilus, whose name is authentic and not a pseudo-nym, was born in Moscow on 25 August (old style) 1862, the son of a minor noble landowner.[4] Nilus' ancestors on his father's side were Lutheran and came from the Baltics, which explains his non-Russian last name – a deriva-tion from Nicholas. Nilus' father was the first to be baptized in the Orthodox rite. His maternal ancestors were Russian landed nobility. Nilus studied law at the University of Moscow, worked briefly in the judicial system, but soon left the state service. He withdrew to his estate in the Orël district, which he managed ineffectively in the old-fashioned, patriarchal way.

Although Nilus had always been indifferent to religion, toward the end of the century he succumbed to the apocalyptic mood that was taking hold of the country. He thus joined those victims of rapid modernization and secularization who identified the downfall of their own world with the end of the world in general. On his pilgrimages, Nilus met the charismatic parish priest and wonder-worker John (Ioann) of Kronstadt (1829–1909, canonized 1990). From these experiences he fashioned his own mystical-apocalyptic faith based on miracles and signs.

Nilus became active as a writer. From October 1907 to May 1912, he lived together with his wife Elena Aleksandrovna (1854–1938) and his former mistress Natal'ia Afanas'evna Volodimerova (1845–1932) near the Optina Pustyn' monastery, renowned as the centre of Russian Orthodox eldership. He worked in the monastery's archives and interacted with the elders (*startsy*). It was during this time that most of his writing and publish-ing *œuvre* was created, including the diary *On the Banks of God's River*, a kind of chronicle of the monastic life at Optina. Other works deal with the lives of Egyptian desert fathers and Russian hermits, describe encounters with monastic elders, miracle-workers and "holy fools" (*iurodivye*), and tell of divination dreams, prophecies and the activities of demonic powers.

Nilus won great fame among Orthodox believers for discovering and editing the teachings and apocalyptic prophecies ascribed to Serafim of Sarov (1754–1833), an ascetic hermit who became one of Russia's most popular saints. Nilus' own description of the circumstances under which he supposedly found those records shortly before Serafim's canonization in 1903 – in a basket with old papers at an attic – and his somehow "miraculously" deciphering them sound highly implausible and resemble the mystifications surrounding the *Protocols*. In both cases, the "originals" – if they ever existed – have been lost (Hagemeister 1998).

Nilus published Serafim's teachings in 1903 in his devotional book *The Great in the Small: Impressions of One's Own and Others' Lives. Notes of an Orthodox Believer*. In the second edition of this book, printed at Tsarskoe Selo in December 1905 with a new subtitle, *And the Antichrist as an Imminent Political Possibility*, Nilus took up *The Protocols of the Elders of Zion* for the first time (Nilus 1905: 325–394). Later editions of his book, also containing the *Protocols*, appeared under various titles in 1911 and 1912. The last edition was published in January 1917, a few weeks before

Figure 5.2 Optina Pustyn' monastery, early May 1909. Standing from left: unknown boy, Elena Nilus, Alexandre du Chayla, landlady; seated from left: Sergei Nilus, unknown girl, Natal'ia Volodimerova. (Private collection M. Hagemeister.)

the fall of the monarchy in Russia, by the famous Holy Trinity Monastery at Sergiev Posad and bore the menacing title, borrowed from Matthew 24:33 and Mark 23:29, *"It Is Near, Even at the Doors"*: *Concerning That Which People Do Not Wish to Believe and Which Is So Near* (1917).

Nilus the apocalypticist

In his commentary, Nilus interpreted the *Protocols* within the framework of his apocalyptic worldview – as the unveiling of a hidden strategy of the satanic forces of darkness and their worldly allies, Jews and Masons, in their unremitting struggle against the divine forces of light (embodied in the Russian Orthodox Church), a struggle which seemed to have entered its final stage at the turn of the century. Nilus felt deeply apocalyptic and was convinced of an ordered world, in which God and other supernatural agents exercised significant influence and control. He constantly noticed signs that the end was fast approaching; he regularly believed he saw the "Seal of the Antichrist" or the "Number of the Beast" around him.[5] This belief that the end was nigh Nilus shared with many of his contemporaries who, like him, saw the breakdown and dissolution of the old order and traditional customs – consequences of the political, economic and social upheavals that shook Russia at the beginning of the twentieth century – through the prism of religion: as a foreboding of an imminent eschatological catastrophe and as evidence of the work of the Antichrist and his allies.[6]

Doomsday scenarios and the fear of revolution received special treatment in the subculture of Russian Judeophobia. The premodern or antimodern consciousness saw Jews and Freemasons – sponsors and beneficiaries of progress and enlightenment – as the henchmen of the Antichrist; indeed, they were often identified with him.[7] Thus, the common denominator of apocalyptic concepts blended anti-Jewish myths with fashionable occultism and the belief in – or even personal encounter with – demonic forces. The border between fiction and reality was often nebulous, and mystifications were not easily recognizable to many.

Nilus seems to have been favourably impressed by the famous *Short Tale of the Antichrist*, the last work of the renowned philosopher and alleged philosemite Vladimir Solov'ëv (1853–1900), published in 1900. With his vision of the Antichrist as "the coming man", Solov'ëv, in his own words, wanted "to reveal in advance the deceptive mask behind which the abyss of evil is hiding" (Solov'ëv 1988: 643). His declared goal was to warn people of the growing covert and seductive power of evil in history and to call for a fight against it (for this reason he read the *Tale* in public). He did indeed achieve this goal, whereby the *Tale* was widely perceived not as a work of fiction but as a concrete apocalyptic prophecy and warning. Solov'ëv

Figure 5.3 Frontispiece to Sergei Nilus, *Near Are the Coming Antichrist and the Kingdom of the Devil on Earth*, Sergiev Posad 1911, with the text of the *Protocols*. All illustrations are from Eliphas Lévi, *Dogme et rituel de la haute magie* (Paris 1856). In the centre is an image of the Antichrist, the false Messiah of the Jews and coming ruler of the world, which appears in Lévi as a reproduction of the "*Chariot d'Hermes*" on the 7th card of the Tarot. Nilus interpreted the monogram TAROT as "Talmudi Adveniens Rex Orbis Terrarum". The Tetragrammaton (*le Pentagramme de Faust*) and the Seal of Solomon (*le Triangle de Salomon*), which Nilus interpreted as the "Seal of the Antichrist", also come from Lévi, while the "*quatre grands noms cabalistiques*" became for him the "symbolic formula of the 'Secret Power of Lawlessness'". Above all these Satanic signs, Nilus placed the cross of Orthodoxy with the inscription "In this you will be victorious". (Private collection M. Hagemeister.)

depicted the Antichrist – whom the Jews recognize as the Messiah – as a charismatic "superman" and "benefactor" who gains world power with the help of the "mighty brotherhood of the Freemasons" (Solov'ëv 1988: 745) and the *Comité permanent universel* (which in a Judeophobic reading would stand for the *Alliance Israélite Universelle*, the "central kahal for universal Jewry"), and builds his earthly reign on the promise of universal "peace and security" (*eirēnē kai aspháleia*, 1 Thess 5:3). In Nilus' understanding, this was a visionary revelation of the satanic "Judeo-Masonic world conspiracy" and its goal, the foundation of a Jewish world kingdom as a diabolical perversion of the Kingdom of God. Nilus interpreted Solov'ëv's early and sudden death merely five months after the publication of his *Short Tale of the Antichrist* in a manner similar to Solov'ëv's own premonitions: the revenge of that same dark and sinister force whose secret plans he had exposed in his tale (Nilus 1905: 317–318; Velichko 1903: 171–172). However, the actual "proof" of the accuracy of Solov'ëv's prophecy was, for Nilus, to be found in the *Protocols* (Nilus 1905: 316–319, 321–322).[8] The Jewish king whom the "Elders" want to install is none other than the Antichrist himself:

> There is no doubt about it! On the apostate world, with all the power and authority of Satan, looms the universal threat of the kingdom of the triumphant Sanhedrin of Israel: The King, born of the blood of Zion, the Antichrist, is close to the throne of world domination.
>
> (Nilus 1905: 405)

We see, therefore, that Nilus interpreted the *Protocols* not primarily in a political framework – the interpretation that dominated in later years – but placed them in a religious, eschatological context: as *apokálypsis*, that is, the unveiling or uncovering of the struggle between the forces of Good and Evil, both in their invisible otherworldly incarnations and in their visible earthly allies.[9] For the interpretation of the eschatological events, there was no need for authentic documents and certain facts; rather, the eschatological imagination decided on the correctness of the sources. Their authenticity was thus ultimately irrelevant (Nilus 1905: 323). Nilus is said to have remarked to a sceptic in pious simplicity:

> Let us assume that the "Protocols" are inauthentic. Can't God also reveal the impending lawlessness through them? Did not Balaam's ass prophesy? Can't God turn dog bones into miraculous relics for the sake of our faith? So can he make even a liar proclaim the truth.
>
> (Du Chayla 1921b: 5)[10]

For Nilus, even if the *Protocols* themselves were a forgery, they nevertheless testified to a higher truth.

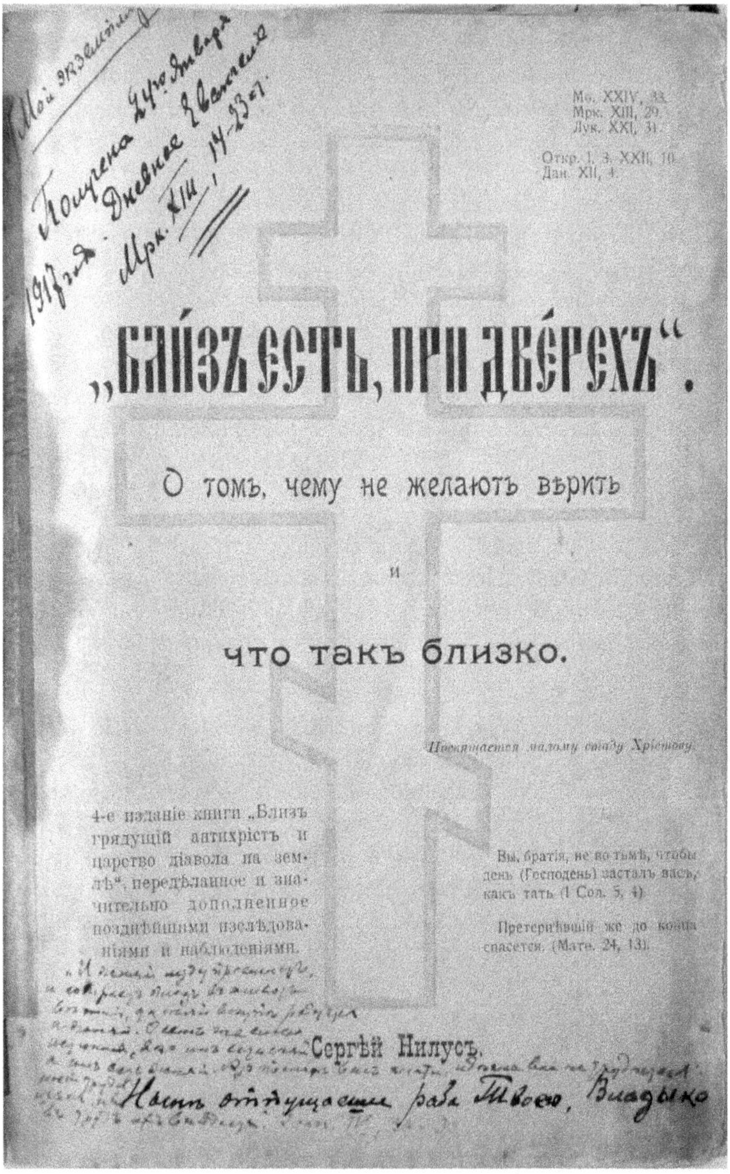

Figure 5.4 Title page of Sergei Nilus, *"It Is Near, Even at the Doors"*, Sergiev
Posad 1917, with the text of the *Protocols*. Nilus' personal copy, in the
upper left corner reception note "24 January 1917". (Private collection
M. Hagemeister.)

One could, correctly, criticize us for the apocryphal nature of this document [the *Protocols*; M.H.]. But if it were possible to prove its authenticity by way of documentation or trustworthy witnesses; if one could reveal the faces of those sitting at the top of the world conspiracy, pulling the bloodied strings, then the very "mystery of lawlessness" would be broken which must remain intact until his incarnation as the "son of perdition".

(Nilus 1905: 323)

Nilus' reference here is to the famous revelation in the second letter of Paul to the Thessalonians, telling of the appearance of the Antichrist himself, who is expected soon, before the *parousia*, the Second Coming, of Christ:

for that day will not come, unless the rebellion comes first, and the man of lawlessness is revealed, the son of perdition, who opposes and exalts himself against every so-called god or object of worship, so that he takes his seat in the temple of God, proclaiming himself to be God. ... For the mystery of lawlessness is already at work.

(*2 Thess* 2:3-4, 7)

The "mystery of lawlessness" was, for Nilus, indeed already at work. He saw the threatening signs everywhere; however, the time was not ripe, for the adversary had yet to appear and reveal his wickedness. His power was still being muzzled by a delaying, inhibitory, restraining power, by what Paul's letter calls the *katechon*. Much has been speculated about the mysterious figure of the *katechon* (see Chapter 6). For Nilus it was evident that the only power capable of repelling the Antichrist was Holy Russia − the autocratic power of the Tsar and the Orthodox monasteries, bulwarks against the swelling flood of godlessness (Nilus 1909).

The drama of salvation

Russians and Jews were, for Nilus, the peoples of the *éschaton*, the end of time: The role of the Jews in the history of salvation (*Heilsgeschichte*) included, whether they knew it or not, struggling against Christianity and striving for world power, exactly as the *Protocols* revealed. This plan for world domination had, according to Nilus, been crafted by Solomon and other Jewish sages as early as 929 BCE and was, over time, continuously amended and elaborated by the initiated. The apostle Paul, one of the most promising students of the Pharisees in his time, was surely also initiated into the plan, and it was *precisely this plan* that he meant when he referred to the "mystery of lawlessness" that was "already at work" (Nilus 1917: 161).

Figure 5.5 Page from Nilus' personal copy of his 1917 edition of the *Protocols* with handwritten additions. The upper illustration shows the depiction of "Baphomet" designed by Éliphas Lévi, an idol figure allegedly worshipped by the Grand Masters of the Order of the Templars and later by the Freemasons, who is also interpreted as the Antichrist. Above it, by Nilus' hand: "The abomination that makes desolate (Dan. XI, 31; XII, 11)". (Private collection M. Hagemeister.)

Nilus wanted to warn his Christian brothers of this "deadly danger that was fast approaching".

Nilus was no racist antisemite, unlike, for example, Father Pavel Florenskii (1882–1937), the highly revered Orthodox priest and philosopher, who identified the Jews in racial terms as the enemies of the Aryans and as the polluters of the blood of other races and who proposed the castration of all Jews (which, however, as a Christian, he had to reject) (Hagemeister and Metelka 2001). Nilus, by contrast, shared the traditional views of Christian anti-Judaism, according to which the *perfidi Judaei*, who refused to recognize Jesus as their Messiah, have to play a central, predetermined role in the cosmic drama of passion and salvation, namely as pathbreakers and agents of the Antichrist who compete with God for rule over the world. Nevertheless, they always remain within the divine plan; indeed, they function as tools of God, so that their enmity is necessary and salvific. Just as Judas's betrayal enabled the son of God to die a redeeming death (for which reason Christians also pray for Judas's salvation), so the Jews' actions help propel the historical process toward the final redemption. Nilus perceived a tragic dimension to this negative role that the Jews had thrust upon them. Just as other millenarians, he believed that their fateful part had to be played out according to the pre-ordained divine plan until the end of history. At the end of the age – after a brief reign of the Antichrist – the Jews, or the better part of them, will inevitably recognize and repent of their apostasy, turn away from the Antichrist, the ruler of this world, and accept the true Messiah whose "kingdom is not of this world" (*John* 18:36), at which time "all Israel will be saved" (*Rom* 11:26). Therefore, the Jews must be preserved. It is, after all, their conversion that will precipitate the Second Coming of Christ and the salvation of the world. Until that time, however, Jews in their impenitence and rebellion are to blame for the suffering in the world and must themselves suffer the wrath of God. All of which means that they can be despised and oppressed but not physically destroyed, especially since, at the end of time, God's initial love will greet them once more.

Christian anti-Judaism, despite its cruel tendencies, did not have the physical destruction of Jewry as its aim.[11] Nilus expressly appealed to his readers not to harbour enmity towards "the Jewish people, who, still blinded in their ardent and fiery – although false – belief, are not to blame for the satanic sins of their leaders: the scribes and Pharisees who have once before led Israel to ruin" (Nilus 1905: 323). "It is not the people of God who are to blame for the satanic sin of the war against God, it is their secret Sanhedrin who is to blame" (ibid.: 417).

For Nilus, as for many other Russian religious thinkers, the "final solution" of the so-called "Jewish question" lies in *conversion*, that is, the elimination of Judaism, rather than of Jews (cf. Rossman 2002: 211–220;

Невѣрующіе во Іисуса Христа Іудеи примутъ антихриста за Мессію (Іоан. 5, 43; 2-е Сол. 2, 10—12).

Figure 5.6 "The Jews who do not believe in Jesus Christ accept the Antichrist as the Messiah (*John* 5:43; 2 *Thess* 2:10–12)". Illustration from *Znameniia prishestviia Antikhrista* (Signs of the Coming of the Antichrist), Moscow 1912.

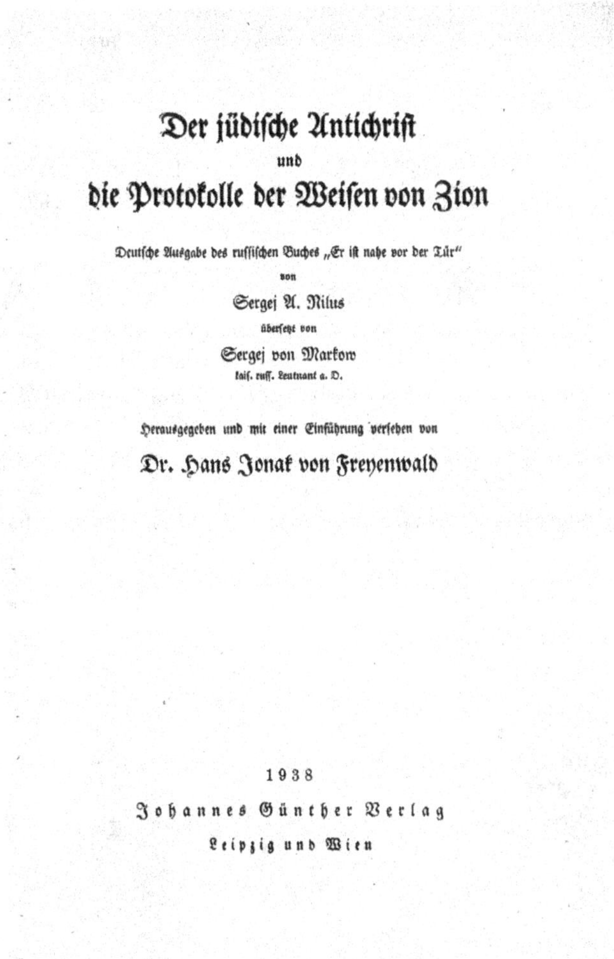

Der jüdische Antichrist

und

die Protokolle der Weisen von Zion

Deutsche Ausgabe des ruſſiſchen Buches „Er iſt nahe vor der Tür"

von

Sergej A. Nilus

überſetzt von

Sergej von Markow
kaiſ. ruſſ. Leutnant a. D.

Herausgegeben und mit einer Einführung verſehen von

Dr. Hans Jonak von Freyenwald

1938

Johannes Günther Verlag

Leipzig und Wien

Figure 5.7 Title page of an unpublished German translation of Sergei Nilus'
edition of the *Protocols* (1938). Nilus' apocalyptic interpretation
of the *Protocols* found no place in the German National Socialist's
antisemitic concept. A German edition of his book with the title *The
Jewish Antichrist and the Protocols of the Elders of Zion* was ready for
publication in 1938 when Nazi censorship prevented its publication
because of the "lengthy comments ... on religious topics". Previously,
the Nazi Party's (NSDAP) central publishing house had already refused
to publish it. Hans Jonak von Freyenwald to Sergei Sergeevich Nilus, 5
May 1939, Wiener Collection, University of Tel Aviv: Bern Trial, box
16/-; the library holds both the manuscript of the translation and the
proof-sheets. See Hagemeister (2017: 121–122, 390–391).

Horowitz 2017: 198–214).[12] Nilus saw in the *Protocols* a text that seemed to validate his Christian-apocalyptic worldview. The transition from Christian anti-Judaism to the Nazis' murderous antisemitism was to a large extent fluent – even Goebbels spoke of Jewry as "the Antichrist of world history". But still: Nilus expected the salvation of all of Israel; Goebbels intended the extermination of all Jews.

From 1912 to 1917 Nilus lived in Valdai, then until 1923 in Linovitsa (government of Poltava) on the estate of Prince Vladimir Zhevakhov (1875–1938). Here, too, Nilus was active as a writer and kept up a lively correspondence. Nilus regarded the Bolshevik Revolution, which to him seemed to bear out the plan of the "Elders of Zion", as an eschatological catastrophe and the beginning of the reign of the Antichrist, the false messiah of the Jews, who instead of the Heavenly Jerusalem promised paradise on Earth.

Nilus declined to leave Russia, instead joining the "Catacomb Church", the underground movement of Russian Orthodoxy that refused to compromise with the Bolsheviks. Together with his wife, he moved from place to place, living mostly in Ukraine. Arrested several times, tried, and imprisoned, he was always released, even though his identity was known to the

Figure 5.8 Sergei Nilus in his study, Linovitsa. Photograph of an officer during the occupation of Ukraine by German troops in the summer of 1918. (Private collection M. Hagemeister.)

authorities. Finally, utterly destitute, he found refuge with a parish priest in the village of Krutets, some 80 miles northeast of Moscow. There, on 14 January 1929, he died of a heart attack. His only son, Sergei (1883–1941) went to Poland after the Revolution of 1917. During the Bern trial (1933–1935) in which the *Protocols* was condemned as a fraud, he acted as an expert witness by sending a report that vouched for the authenticity of the book (Hagemeister 2017: 484–492).

Following the end of the Soviet Union, Nilus has become a cult figure among Orthodox fundamentalists and nationalists (Hagemeister 2006). His books are regularly republished, often under the benediction of local Orthodox Church authorities, and can be found in church bookshops in even the most distant provinces (Shnirel'man 2017: 145–152).

While in the West Nilus is portrayed as a mysterious agent or a crazy monk who roams through conspiracy stories, in Russia he is held in the highest esteem as a religious writer. There, too, his name remains inextricably linked with *The Protocols of the Elders of Zion*, which are sometimes interpreted as an apocalypse, sometimes as a political pamphlet, and sometimes as both at once.

Notes

1 For a critical discussion, see Hagemeister (2008a).
2 Pious readers saw in Eco's novel the secret announcement of the birth of the Antichrist and interpreted the author's name as the abbreviation of a satanic incantation: "Ego Conficio Oraculum" (I fulfil the prophecy [of the end of the world]).
3 Unfortunately, the results of careful research are only slowly being taken note of. In an authoritative study of the *Protocols*, Stephen E. Bronner still writes that Nilus was "the son of Swiss émigrés who had entered Russia during the reign of Peter I" (Bronner 2019: 62).
4 For Nilus' biography as well as for literature by and about him, see Bagdasarov and Fomin (1995); Polovinkin (1995); Hagemeister (1991, 2003, 2005a, 2005b). See also Chapter 6 in this volume.
5 For Nilus, the "Seal of the Antichrist" was connected with the "Number of the Beast" in the hexagonal "Shield of David" (*Magen David*). Nilus expected the appearance of the (then 30-year-old) Antichrist in 1912, since the famous elder Amvrosii in Optina monastery had announced his birth in 1882.
6 For a general survey on apocalypticism in Russia at the turn of the century, see Billington (1966: 504–518); Bethea (1989); Clay (1998); Katsis (2000); *Ėskhatologicheskii sbornik* (2006).
7 See Dudakov (1993); Isupov (1995). On Russian Judeophobia, see Löwe (1993); Klier (1995, 1998). As Johannes Heil (2006) has shown, the narrative of the "Jewish world conspiracy" and the Jews as allies of the Antichrist goes back to the thirteenth century, but was gradually desacralized in the West in the process of secularization; the "enemies of God" became the "enemies of humanity".

8 For the remarkable parallels between the content of Solov'ёv's *Short Tale of the Antichrist* and the *Protocols*, see Hagemeister (2000, 2010).

9 Dudakov (1993: 154–155) pointed out that in his editions, Nilus had placed a short summary of the contents before each of the protocols, the specific points of which he then repeated in the margins next to the text. This was not only to facilitate the reader's orientation, but also to underline the "apocalyptic" image of the *Protocols* by presenting them in a style similar to the texts of the Bible. As far as I am aware, only the Orthodox theologian Anton Kartashёv (1875–1960) refers to the *Protocols* as apocalypse. His 1923 foreword to a critical study, today almost forgotten, describes them as a "faked apocalypse" but does not elaborate on the idea (Kartashёv, 1923).

10 Whether the quotation is authentic must remain open, but it marks Nilus' belief in the *Protocols* as a revelation of salvation history, since the "truth" of biblical statements is not based on their historicity either.

11 This is stressed by Katz (2001: 24–27, 42–45). Referring to the Christian expectation of the "salvation of Israel" (even if only in the *eschaton*), the author argues against the "influential and widespread argument ... that there was an essential continuity between Christian and Nazi antisemitism", since only the latter aimed at the annihilation of the Jewish people.

12 Thus, even on his deathbed, Vladimir Solov'ёv prayed for the conversion of the Jews, i.e. the abandonment of their religion and identity in order to establish a Christian theocracy (see Horowitz 2017: 211–214). The Russian philosopher Nikolai Berdiaev (1874–1948) declared: "The final solution of the Jewish question is only possible from an eschatological perspective. This will also be the fateful resolution of world history, in the final struggle between Christ and Antichrist" (Berdiaev 1923: 128). And Aleksei Losev (1893–1988), a Christian Neoplatonist and one of the most prominent figures in Russian philosophical and religious thought of the twentieth century, called historical Judaism the "stronghold of global Satanism" (Anon. 1996: 122). In contrast, a biologistic-materialistic racism, such as that espoused by Florenskii, does not permit belief in the transforming effect of the sacrament of baptism: conversion does not help here, evil must be destroyed.

6 The Third Rome against the Third Temple

Apocalypticism and conspiracism in post-Soviet Russia

The experience of crisis and the fear of catastrophe have led to an upsurge of conspiratorial and apocalyptic interpretations of history in post-Soviet Russia, both of which are marked by sharp dualism and determinism. Based on a long tradition of apocalyptic prophecies and speculations, Holy Russia is presented as the eschatological Third Rome, as *katechon*, called upon and chosen to withstand the Antichrist (who will take his seat in the Third temple in Jerusalem) and his agents. These agents are identified predominantly with the Jews, the alleged supporters and beneficiaries of the modern "West". In ecclesiastical and nationalist circles, this chapter shows, *The Protocols of the Elders of Zion* are perceived as the uncovering of the hidden strategy of the satanic forces of darkness in their unremitting struggle against the divine forces of light. The "apocalyptic matrix" with its eschatologically defined proponents of doom and salvation offers orientation, solidarity and compensation all in one.

Apocalypticism and conspiracism

The view of history as a transcendent or immanent history of passion and salvation is based on the assumption that the historical process has a purpose towards which it is driven by the permanent struggle between two irreconcilable forces – that of good and that of evil – and that historical events acquire their significance only through a pre-determined end, *sub specie finis*.

In the Christian interpretation, the historical process is a meaningful unity insofar as it is grounded in God's plan (Providence), which is revealed to the believers at its beginning (Creation/Fall) and at its end (Doomsday), as well as through key stages (the redemptive death of Jesus Christ). The *télos* of history – at the same time its end and its goal, which is constructive of its meaning – is revealed as a vision in a dream or in ecstasy (*en pneúmati*, Rev 4:2) and recorded in apocalyptic texts. Thus, for example,

DOI: 10.4324/9781003200789-6

the Book of Revelation describes the events at the end of time, the fight between the forces of light and the forces of darkness, the deception or seduction by the Evil One(s), the decisive battle and the Last Judgement, the demise of the old world torn apart by conflicts and the beginning of a new, perfect, and a-temporal one.

Dualism and determinism are also crucial markers of the myth of a world conspiracy. This myth, too, is based on the belief that the course of history is predetermined and that it is advancing towards a final goal, but in this case, both the course and the final goal are defined by conspirators who are presented as omnipotent global agents, their aim being an (unlimited) rule over all of humanity. While the end of history expected by Christians has, of course, been decided upon, and is not subject to human intervention, there is still a chance that the goal pursued by the mysterious masterminds of this world can be averted, if those who have been warned put up proper resistance.

Just like apocalyptic narratives, the conspiracy myth also promises access to a reality that is essentially hidden. But it is exactly there, in the realm of the clandestine, that the decisive events take place, the struggle of the opposites, which drive history forward and towards its end. What has been given to us as reality is but a deceptive apparition; that which really matters is happening in secret, in a domain that is inaccessible to the average person. Only the initiated and those able to interpret the signs can lift the curtain and reach the truth. Even the crudest conspiracy theory claims to reveal this "higher" reality, allowing one to look behind the scenes at "the Hidden Hand" that is pulling the strings on the stage of history. Like other "grand narratives", apocalyptic and conspiracy narratives satisfy the need for an all-embracing interpretation of history and create meaning in an increasingly secular, disenchanted world. Besides, they offer a user manual: friend and foe are clearly distinguishable; the foe is demonized and fought against; the virtuous close ranks. They provide consolation by demonstrating that the time of suffering is limited and that the reign of evil will (or can) be overcome.

In Russia the eschatological conception of history has a long tradition. Lotman and Uspenskii (1984) even identified it as one of the markers of Russian culture. The philosopher Nikolai Berdiaev (1874–1948) called the Russian people "in accordance with their metaphysical nature and vocation in the world a people of the End" and thought the apocalyptic vision a fundamental national feature (Berdyaev 1947: 193).[1] Every so often the collective imagination would become inflamed in a mixture of terror and hope, as revelations and prophecies were made about the end of history and the figure of the Antichrist, the "deceiver" and "the ruler of this world", as well as about the messianic role of Russia in the plan of the Christian salvation history (*Heilsgeschichte*) (Billington 1966: 504–518; Bethea 1989; Clay 1998; Katsis 2000).

The highest point of eschatological tension in modern Russia was the late nineteenth and early twentieth centuries, as radical political, economic, and social changes – the results of accelerated industrialization, urbanization, and secularization – shook the country. These events were often interpreted with the help of religious categories: as a foreboding of an imminent eschatological catastrophe and as evidence of the hidden destructive work of the Antichrist and his allies (see Chapter 5).

Even today, after the failure of secular belief in progress with its promise of a "radiant future" or "paradise on earth", and with its gigantic toll of sacrifices, there is a tendency to elevate the great catastrophes that Russia went through in the twentieth century, as well as present-day crises and conflicts, to the level of salvation history and thus fill them with meaning. Much research has been done on the enormous significance of the "apocalyptic matrix" for post-Soviet Russia's conception of itself (Akhmetova 2005, 2010; Bagdasarian 2006; Beglov 2014; Bessonov 2014; Levkievskaia 2005; Mitrokhin 2007; Shnirel'man 2017).[2] However, the connection between apocalyptic and conspiratorial ideas is yet to be more closely examined (on conspiracism in post-Soviet Russia, see Yablokov 2018; Borenstein 2019; Livers 2020).

The apocalyptical reading of *The Protocols of the Elders of Zion*

The present-day evocations of the hidden activities of the Antichrist and his agents can rely on a broad range of prophecies and their theological, philosophical, as well as folkloristic, literary, and political interpretations. Alongside the classical theological works, such as Aleksandr Beliaev's (1898) monumental study on *Godlessness and the Antichrist*, which has been made accessible again as a reprint, or Boris Molchanov's (1938) *The Mystery of Lawlessness and the Antichrist*, as well as more recent scholarly treatises and anthologies, is the rich tradition of (apocryphal) apocalyptic writings, which are distributed in mass editions and quoted again and again. There is, however, one text that has been the default source of reference for both apocalypticists and conspiracy theorists, and not only in Russia: *The Protocols of the Elders of Zion*.

First published in Russia in 1903, the *Protocols* is an anonymous work that purports to be the literal transcript of one or several speeches given by an anonymous Jew at a meeting of undefined people (presumably Jews) at an undisclosed location, at an unknown point in time. The speaker outlines in great detail the secret methods and goals of a century-old Judeo-Masonic conspiracy against the entire non-Jewish world. The aim of the Jewish conspirators, who see themselves as "benefactors" bringing eternal peace and order to the world, is the establishment of a perfectly organized paternalistic dictatorship with a king from the House of David at its helm. This world leader is described as a charismatic father figure, a model of virtue, self-control, and reason. Admired by the masses (both Jews and non-Jews), he is almost idolized. A benevolent despot, the Jewish king will rule over a harmonious albeit dystopian world in which the vast majority of people, being relieved of the burden of freedom, live in dull happiness and quiet. The text of the *Protocols*, based largely on a compilation of literary materials from the second half of the nineteenth century, was in all likelihood written at the beginning of the twentieth century (De Michelis 2004). From the outset, it was presented as a genuine document, often accompanied by elaborate explanations as to how it fell into the hands of the publisher. Despite the most intensive research, the details of its origins still defy clarification. In particular, the question of its authorship still remains open (Hagemeister 2008a; Levy 2014).

Of all publishers and commentators of the *Protocols*, Sergei Nilus (1862–1929), an apocalyptic thinker and prolific religious writer, is still considered most influential (see Chapter 5). Following the end of the Soviet Union, Nilus and his writings have been rediscovered in Russia (Hagemeister 2006). Nilus has become virtually a cult figure among Orthodox fundamentalists and nationalists. His books – especially those that contain the *Protocols* – are regularly republished, often under the benediction of local Orthodox Church authorities, and can be found in church bookshops in even the most distant provinces (Shnirel'man 2017: 145–152). In addition, congresses and annual "Nilus Readings" are held on the anniversary of his death, where self-appointed experts on "Masonology" (*masonovedenie*), "Judeology" (*evreevedenie*) and "Conspirology" (*konspirologiia*) gather. In this milieu, strongly influenced by the religious imagination, the *Protocols* are – quite as Nilus intended – read and understood as an apocalyptic text exposing the hidden machinations of "the talmudic Jewry of the world in the preparation for and establishment of the global reign of the Antichrist" (Shchedrin 2002: 25).

This incorporates the *Protocols* into a long tradition of apocalyptic writings, of which many, like the *Protocols* themselves, are apocryphal. Examples of this genre include the anti-Jewish and anti-Mason prophecies of Saint Serafim of Sarov (1754–1833), composed probably in the second half of the nineteenth century by Russian reactionaries and now distributed under the title *The Antichrist and Russia* (Hagemeister 1998, 2010, 2011a: 464–467), or the *Vision of John of Kronstadt*, a bloodthirsty apocalypse contrived in the early 1920s as anti-Bolshevik propaganda and attributed to the famous miracle worker and clairvoyant of Kronstadt (1829–1909), a friend and kindred spirit of Sergei Nilus: Guided by Serafim, John (Ioann) traverses the realm of Bolshevik terror and watches the triumph and fall of the Jewish world ruler, the Antichrist.[3] As in the case of the *Protocols* and the *Vision of John of Kronstadt*, the true origin of Serafim's eschatological-apocalyptic prophecies remains unexplained to this day, but this does not diminish their popularity. Since the 'miraculous recovery' of his relics in November 1990, and their transfer to the Diveevo monastery in the summer of 1991, Serafim has become Russia's most revered saint, and the apoca-lyptic prophecies attributed to him are widely disseminated, despite their dubious authenticity (Basin 1996; Hagemeister 1998; Garrard and Garrard 2008: 101–140).

A historiosophic interpretation of Russian history

In post-Soviet Russia, "historiosophy" (*istoriosofiia*) and "metahistory" (*metaistoriia*) are popular buzz words referring to attempts to speculatively determine the goal and meaning of the process of world history, the forces and laws that define it, as well as to evaluate all of these as constructive or destructive, propitious or ominous.[4] To this end, the nineteenth- and twen-tieth-century Russian traditions of the metaphysics of history and historical theology (where history appears as a revelation of God's design), as well as the dualistic-deterministic vision of history according to Soviet ideol-ogy (history as a revelation of "the universal laws of social development") are taken up and popularized. After all, in its eschatology and demonology, Marxism was no stranger to a version of history that had an end goal (the "realm of freedom"), the "inner, hidden laws" and "real ultimate driving forces" (Engels 1888: 52, 54) of which disclose themselves only to pro-gressive consciousness. A classic historiosophic interpretation of history that remains in print is the "philosophical poetry" written later in life by Vladimir Solov'ëv (1853–1900). His descriptions of the rise, reign, and fall of the Antichrist had and still have an enormous impact on many Russian intellectuals; they are read and re-read even today not as literary fiction, but as a concrete prophecy, which is interpreted with reference to the present day and the near future (Hagemeister 2010: 261). Other influential sources include the eschatological treatises and "fantasies" of Lev Tikhomirov (1852–1923) (1999b, 2004), a former terrorist turned ultraorthodox mon-archist, as well as the Manichean versions of history developed by the reli-gious philosophers Father Pavel Florenskii (1882–1937) and Aleksei Losev (1893–1988).

Florenskii and Losev, who are among the most prominent figures in Russian metaphysical thought, see the history of humanity in an

eschatological perspective as a battlefield with two opposite cosmic principles fighting each other: Logos and Chaos, Transcendence and Immanence
or, theologically speaking, Christ and the Antichrist (Hagemeister 2001:
29–33, 2016: 28–31). In 1929 Losev wrote an interpretation of world
history at the core of which was the myth of a Judeo-Satanic conspiracy.
According to this vision of history, the historical agents of the Antichrist are
the Jews. Rootless, materialistic, rationalistic and preoccupied with earthly
matters, they lead people astray with their claims to self-salvation and self-
deification. The Renaissance, the Enlightenment, humanism, and liberalism, as well as "the Leviathan of capitalism and socialism" (Anon. 1996:
127), mark the stages of their secret destructive deeds through history, cul-
minating in Marxism and Communism as the most complete expression of
the kabbalistic, Talmudic, Satanical spirit of Judaism: "Judaism with all its
dialectical and historical consequences is Satanism, the stronghold of global
Satanism" (ibid.: 122). The same year in which he wrote these lines, Losev
secretly took monastic oaths and became monk Andronik. Decorated with
insignia and honours of the Soviet state, he died in 1988 in Moscow.

Seen from a historiosophic or metahistorical perspective, the history of
Russia, too, appears to be a field where an "invisible battle" (*nezrimaia
bitva*) is raging between the forces of light and those of darkness. In this
interpretation, historical events are understood as an analogy to Christ's
passion on the Way of the Cross,[5] as an extended act of crucifixion per-
formed by the forces of the Antichrist, and as a sacrifice – which the period
of Soviet rule is frequently associated with (Rossman 2002: 223–225).
According to the proponents of "the sacral metahistory", Russia is presently
lying in a grave, unconscious, but a miraculous resurrection will not be long
in coming (Bagdasarian 2006: 436–437).[6] In the period of prosperity that
will then begin, the last period of world history before the Last Judgement,
the reborn Russia under the guidance of "the Emperor of the Last Days"
will free humanity of the power of evil. Thus, Russia sacrifices itself in
order to triumph in the end.

This vision of Russia's decisive role in the drama of salvation history
is supported by the doctrine of Moscow as the Third Rome, which comes
from the famous formula of the Pskov monk Filofei, who wrote in the first
half of the sixteenth century: "For two Romes have fallen, and the Third
stands, and a fourth shall never be" (Duncan 2000: 11; on the political myth,
see Østbø 2016). After the "break" from Rome (the East-West Schism of
1054) and the "betrayal" of Constantinople (at the heretical Council of
Florence in 1439), Russia becomes the last kingdom of true believers. The
end of this kingdom will also mean the end of history, with the coming of
the Antichrist, the Second Coming of Christ and the establishment of the
Kingdom of God. Until that time, Holy Russia and its rulers remain chosen

by God, destined to ward off the adversary of Christ and withhold the end of the world (Nazarov 2005: 914–955).[7]

In this ethno-theological narrative, the Russian Tsar acts as the *katechon*, that blocking, restraining force to which Paul refers in his Second Epistle to the Thessalonians: "For the mystery of lawlessness is already at work. Only the one who now restrains it [*ho katéchōn*] will do so until he is taken out of the way. And then the lawless one will be revealed" (2 *Thess* 2:7–8).[8] Nicholas II's abdication in March 1917, to which he was forced through "a cowardly betrayal", and his murder in July 1918 were then understood as the realization of that very prophecy, that is, as a removal of the *katechon*, so that the way became free for the reign of the Antichrist, the "future ruler of the Third Temple" (Levkievskaia 2005: 184). The regicide – the second worst crime after deicide – was an "apocalyptic crime" planned over a long time and executed by the agents of the Antichrist (the Jews) according to a "kabbalistic and Masonic ritual" by cutting off the head and having it preserved.[9] The apostle-like ruler of the Third Rome, chosen and anointed by God and holder of "the katechonic Orthodox power", is "objectively the greatest metaphysical foe of Antichrist's Jewish agents", and his elimination was an act "of supreme metaphysical and religious significance", according to the historian Mikhail Nazarov (2005: 213–223).

However, many believers are convinced that the place of the *katechon* is not vacant but occupied by the Mother of God. As proof they cite the miraculous discovery of an icon in the village of Kolomenskoe, near Moscow, on 2 March 1917, the day of Nicholas II's abdication. The icon depicts the seated Queen of Heaven with the symbols of her earthly rule, in imperial purple, with crown, sceptre, and orb. The icon, named "She Who Reigns" (*Derzhavnaia*), was immediately attributed with miraculous properties, and began to attract numerous pilgrims. Copies of it were circulated widely; the image was worshipped in all parts of the country. Even today, it is seen by many as a sign that the protection of Russia from the assault of the Antichrist has been passed over from the Tsar to the Mother of God, and that she will retain the autocratic power until the restoration of the monarchy (Nazarov 2005: 950; Bagdasarian 2006: 441–442).

The murder of the Tsar and his family is considered to be the central event of Russia's twentieth-century history. All the misfortunes and suffering that came later – the persecution of Christians, the famine and the terror, the death of millions of people and finally, the Great Patriotic War – are perceived as divine punishment for the declension of the Russian people from faith and the Judas-like betrayal of their ruler. Just as Jesus surrendered himself to the will of his Heavenly Father and died on Golgotha for the sins of the world, so did the "Martyr-Tsar" give his life as an expiatory sacrifice for the sins of Russia in Yekaterinburg (the Russian

Golgotha).[10] Only when the Russian people have cleaned their land of idols and symbols of godlessness, only when they have renounced the ideas of democracy and political equality, only when they have repented of their collective guilt and atoned for "the most horrible and fatal crime of the twentieth century" – only then will the Tsar come back and Russia will regain its erstwhile glory (Levkievskaia 2005: 183–191; Akhmetova 2010: 245–260; Khizhii 2014). Admittedly, there is some risk that instead of the Anointed One it will be the "Counter-Anointed" (*anti-christos*) who will take possession of the Russian throne. In this case, it would be "the King of Israel", as the numerical equivalent of the Hebrew words *ha-melek le-Israel* is the number of the second Beast of the Apocalypse (Molchanov 1990: 25).[11]

One of the most vehement and influential propagandists of the self-victimization and self-charismatization of Russia in the first post-Soviet years was the Metropolitan Ioann (Ivan Snychev, 1927–1995) of Saint Petersburg, member of the Holy Synod, and the third hierarch in the ranks of the Russian Orthodox Church. In countless articles, pamphlets, and interviews, Ioann evoked the mission of the Third Rome in the salvation history of the world, as "the last stronghold of true faith" in the struggle against the global conspiracy of the anti-Christian forces (Rossman 2002: 221–225). For the Metropolitan, the apocalyptic enemies of Christianity were first of all the "lawless people" – that is, the Jews – harbouring a plan for the realization of their "centuries-old dream of world supremacy" (Ioann 1993a). Their allies are "the global powers behind the scenes", international Freemasonry, the "transnational financial oligarchy", the supporters of Zionism and Marxism, as well as Israel, the United States and their Western European satellites. Reborn in the spirit of Orthodoxy, Russia could resist these evil forces and their doctrines of materialism, liberalism, and democracy, Holy Russia being the earthly pedestal of the Godly Throne, opposite which stands the "Third Temple", the throne of the Antichrist (Ioann 1994: 7).

The task of educating the Russian public about the machinations of "the forces of global evil" has been continued by the Institute for Russian Civilization, founded in Moscow with Ioann's blessing. The Institute's director, amateur historian Oleg Platonov (b. 1950), has become one of the most prolific and influential antisemitic and anti-Masonic authors in post-Soviet Russia (Mjør 2020). In his book series *Russia's Crown of Thorns,* he presents "documents" that should provide evidence for the "secret war of the Judeo-Masonic civilization with the epicentre USA" against Orthodox Russia. Just like Ioann, Platonov also sees the plan for establishing the rule of the Jewish Antichrist laid out in the *Protocols*, the truth having been revealed to the Russian people by the grace of God (2012).

"The Signs of the Times"

With the beginning of *glasnost'* and *perestroika*, that is, with the end of state censorship and state monopoly on information and eventually the collapse of the Soviet Empire, Russian citizens suddenly found themselves overwhelmed by a flood of differing and conflicting political and commercial information. In the 1990s, as free-market reforms and economic shock therapy threw major parts of the population into poverty and ethnic conflicts flared up along the state borders, people were looking for simple and simplifying explanations that also corresponded to familiar (ideological) patterns of thought. Many substituted Church doctrine for the old Soviet ideology, which like some incarnations of Orthodoxy, drew much of its strength from the idea that Russia was surrounded by hostile, alien forces. This was the moment of *les terribles simplificateurs* and their apocalyptic and conspiracist scenarios.

A veritable torrent of writings – including reprints of pre-revolutionary publications – swept over Russia, in which the secret activities of dark supernatural forces and their earthly allies (Jews, Masons, Zionists, Mondialists and many others) were "revealed" and identified. The concoctions bore titles such as *Invisible Empires*, *Secret Forces*, *The Ideology of the "Mystery of Lawlessness"*, *The Antichrist in Moscow*, *The War Against the Antichrist*, *Attention: The Seal of the Antichrist!*, *The Russian Apocalypse and the End of History* or simply *Conspiracy Against Russia*. Using a range of sources, not least those of the Russian Old Believers (*starovery*) and sectarians, these texts revived and updated centuries-old eschatological, demonological and anti-Jewish representations of the Antichrist, who would be a Jew from the tribe of Dan and become the false Messiah of the Jews; they also talked of the "seal of the Antichrist" and the "number of the Beast".

The readers of these texts learnt that the Antichrist was born in Israel in 1962 and made his appearance in 1992 (Akhmetova 2005: 231, Bagdasarian 2006: 436).[12] For this purpose, the members of the Jewish tribe of Dan were brought from Ethiopia to Israel (Nazarov 2005: 919). Organ transplantation, genetic engineering and cloning, conducted by sinister Masonic and Jewish doctors, secretly served to facilitate the artificial conception of the Antichrist (Nazarov 2005: 922; Akhmetova 2008: 14–18, 2010: 61–65). Likewise, the mummification of Lenin's body and its public display as a "pseudorelic" is denounced as an expression of the cult of the Antichrist, and brought in connection with *Teraphim*, idols, allegedly used by the Israelites in abominable cultic rites. The authors also reveal that the mausoleum on the Red Square was based on the design of the Pergamon Altar, Satan's sacred shrine (Fomin 1993). After the Jews seized Jerusalem in 1967, they secretly set up the "Third Temple", the future residence of the Antichrist, on

the site of the Dome of the Rock and the Al-Aqsa mosque (Fomin 2002a; cf. 2 Thess 2:4).[13]
The belief in the secret undertakings of anti-Christian powers gave rise to a nearly paranoiac obsession with signs. The "seal of the Antichrist", it is claimed, is either implanted as a microchip into the forehead and the right hand of new-born babies, or else a laser is used to tattoo it under the skin, so that people can be controlled and manipulated all their lives (in Russian *zombirovanie* and *kodirovanie*) through a gigantic super-computer, dubbed "The Beast", allegedly based in Brussels (Akhmetova 2010: 145–148; Bessonov 2014: 244–249; Panchenko 2016). In this magical mind-set, the individual taxpayer's number is in fact "the seal of the Antichrist", which comes to replace one's baptismal name in the "book of life" (*Rev* 20:12), thus robbing its bearers of their Christian identity and making them defenceless in the face of anti-Christian forces, which already control the global computer network (Bagdasarian 2006: 444–449; Mitrokhin 2007: 239–244; Akhmetova 2010: 182–186).[14] For the adherents of these theories, the "number of the Beast", without which "no man might buy or sell" (*Rev* 13:17), is also recognisable on bar codes and credit cards (Nazarov 2005: 921; Bagdasarian 2006: 443–444; Bessonov 2014: 246).[15] Those willing to see and to listen had it revealed to them by divine grace that even the most mundane concepts and symbols of the present day also carry secret messages of the Antichrist and his allies, Jews and Masons. Thus, the word *president* is translated as "initiated" (meaning "into Masonry"); *revolution* (pronounced in Russian as *revoliu-tsiia*) actually means "Zionist revolt"; *democracy* denotes the power of the demons, and *demonstration* is a procession of demons. In the word *computer* the "com" stands for "Communist", and "ter" for a "devouring beast" (téras) in Ancient Greek (Akhmetova 2008: 10–13).

The striving for a New World Order, a world government, and a global currency, together with the World Wide Web and the heresy of ecumenism, have, in this worldview, served the establishment of a uniform world religion and global governance in the form of a totalitarian anti-Christian ideocracy (Gavriushin 1991; Bagdasarian 2006: 437–443). The "religious occupation" by foreign sects, together with the growing influence of occultism, Satanism, cosmism, theosophy, and New Age movements have been encouraging apostasy, thus bringing the coming of the Antichrist closer (Ioann 1993b; Akhmetova 2010: 188–189). Feminism, homosexuality, and sorcery are also interpreted eschatologically as "signs of the times" (*Matt* 16:3) on a par with the appearance of demonic creatures in the shape of UFOs and aliens (Kozlov 1990), as well as the growth in the number of "mystical crimes" (*misticheskie prestupleniia*) the latter being a reference to "ritual murders" of Christians (Akhmetova 2010: 189).[16] The Covid-19 pandemic that broke out

СИОНСКИЕ
ПРОТОКОЛЫ

Figure 6.1 The Antichrist as the inspirer of the "Judeo-Masonic World Conspiracy". Title page of an edition of *The Protocols of the Elders of Zion* (Moscow 1993). The illustration depicts Baphomet, designed by Éliphas Lévi, who is identified with the Antichrist.

ЭЛЕМЕНТЫ

ЕВРАЗИЙСКОЕ ОБОЗРЕНИЕ

№2, 1992   Цена свободная

НОВЫЙ МИРОВОЙ ПОРЯДОК

* Юрий Мамлеев, художник иных миров
* Жак Аттали идеолог мондиализма
* Технологический вампиризм
* С.Бабурин: «Тайна России»

ДОСЬЕ: Новый Мировой Порядок в Югославии

Figure 6.2 The Antichrist as Lord of the New World Order. Title page of Aleksandr Dugin's Journal *Élementy* (1992).

at the beginning of 2020 also serves the coming reign of the Antichrist, since "the Jews" announced "the inoculation of diseases" in their *Protocols* as one of the methods to achieve world domination (Nilus 1911: 91; Katasonov 2020). Finally, geopolitical, and ecological catastrophes point to the approaching end of time; it suffices to mention the bombing of the Orthodox brotherly nation of Serbia by NATO forces, the American occupation of Iraq (the apocalyptic Babylon, the Antichrist's "classical" birthplace), or the nuclear accident at Chernobyl, which in Russian means "wormwood", evoking the falling star in Revelation (*Rev* 8:11) (Bagdasarian 2006: 435–442).

In 1993 the publishing house of the Holy Trinity Lavra in Sergiev Posad, the seat of the Moscow Theological Academy, brought out an anthology of apocalyptic visions and eschatological writings. Entitled *Russia Before the Second Coming (of Christ)*, the publication included a wide selection of writings, from those authored by church fathers to modern conspiracist texts, including *The Antichrist and Russia* by Serafim of Sarov, *The Vision of John of Kronstadt*, and *The Protocols of the Elders of Zion*. The original print-run was 100,000 copies. The anthology, published with a foreword by the abbot Isaia and with the financial support of the International Bank of the Cathedral of Christ the Saviour, has become a bestseller. As of today, it is available in numerous official reprints and in even more pirated editions, having expanded to two large-format volumes (Fomin and Fomina 1998; Shnirel'man 2017: 152–171). Apparently, the teachings of the secret activities of the Evil One have obscured the "Good News" of the Gospel.[17]

Also popular in post-Soviet Russia is the apocalyptic œuvre of the American priest-monk and wonderworker Seraphim (Eugene D. Rose, 1934–1982). At the beginning of the 1960s, Rose had come to Orthodoxy under the influence of Helen Kontsevich (1893–1989), Sergei Nilus's niece, and in 1967 had retreated with like-minded people into the forest solitude of northern California.[18] There he lived in abrupt renunciation of the modern world and in the near expectation of the end times, whose prodigies and agents operating in secret he believed to perceive everywhere (Seraphim 2003; Damascene 1993: 637–663). His interpretation of UFOs as contemporary manifestations of demons who, disguised as angels of light, sought to seduce people before the end, became particularly influential (Seraphim 1991, 1996).[19] After his untimely death, Seraphim became a cult figure in Orthodox fundamentalist circles in the USA and Russia, where his apocalyptic writings are widely circulated in translation. Reports of miracles and the depiction of his person on icons testify to the fact that he is already considered a saint by some (Sedgwick 2004: 208–209).

Metaphysical conspiracy theories in post-Soviet Russia – three examples

Aleksandr Dugin: The occult "War of the Continents"

Probably the most comprehensive interpretation of world events according to the scheme of apocalyptic dualism is offered by the self-taught polyglot and well-read "metaphysician" and geopolitician Aleksandr Dugin (b. 1962), from 2008 to 2014 professor at Moscow State University and director of its Centre for Conservative Studies. Since the early 1990s, Dugin, himself a member (since 1999) of the apocalyptically inspired Old Believer Church, has been spreading a mixture of eschatology with esotericism and elements of European and Islamic traditionalism (Sedgwick 2004: 221–237) through multiple channels: the radio programme "Finis mundi", the publishing house Arktogaia, in journals and websites in various languages, as well as in talk shows and interviews on the state-controlled television. According to Dugin, the history of humanity has been determined by an "occult planetary struggle" of two antagonistic powers, the "great war of the continents": land against sea, Behemoth against Leviathan, the organic "tellurocracies" of the East, which are rooted in their native soil, against the rootless and soulless, materialistic "thalassocracies" of the West, that apocalyptic Beast of the Sea (*Rev* 13:1–10).[20]

The United States as the "quintessence of the West" is the empire of the Antichrist, a chimerical, transplanted civilization devoid of any sacral tradition (its self-elevation to "God's New Israel" and "New Zion" – the Anglo-American interpretation of the doctrine of substitution – is for Dugin an especially perfidious attempt at deception by the "Western Antichrist"). The year of the discovery of America (1492 is the year 7000 in the Old Russian-Byzantine calendar, which corresponds to the seventh and last day of creation) marks the "New World" as belonging to the end of time, as does the "sacral geography", which puts paradise in the East where the sun rises, while hell ("the land of the dead") is in the West where the sun sets (Dugin 1999: 645–670). The katechonic powers of Holy Russia, the Third Rome, have been standing against the Antichrist since time immemorial (Dugin 1997: 52–59, 1999: 378–395, 493–521). In order to continue performing its salvationist historical mission for the benefit of humanity, Russia must create a mighty sacral Eurasian empire as a shield against the common archenemy, the modern secular world and the Western materialist, universalist, and all-levelling civilization being the utmost expression of global evil. Russian Old Believers, ultraorthodox Jews, European traditionalists as well as those Islamic fundamentalists who recognize the United States as *al-Dajjâl*, the false messiah, against whom *al-Mahdî*, the prophesied redeemer, will go on a crusade (Dugin 2005) – all of them will be allies in the apocalyptic "final and conclusive battle" or "Endkampf" (Dugin always writes this last word in German).

Arkadii Maler: Russia – the "Northern Katechon"

Dugin's work, with its provocative mix of esoteric and aggressively anti-Western motives, finds particular resonance among young intellectuals, some of whom have followed in his footsteps. One of them is the self-proclaimed "Orthodox mystic" Arkadii Maler (b. 1979), a vehement propagandist of a "political Orthodoxy" and a leading ideologue of the anti-Western "neo-Byzantine" doctrine.[21] In his book *The Spiritual Mission of the Third Rome*, Maler declares that Russia is "the northern *katechon*", evoking, like Dugin, Russia's "eschatological mission" to fulfil its "central katechonic role" in the fight against the New World Order of "the godless West", with its materialism, liberalism, and moral relativism (Maler 2005: 134–136, 170–206, 2007: 110–124).[22] According to Maler, even the Bolsheviks, and in particular Stalin, unconsciously pursued this goal when they made Moscow the capital of the "Red Empire" and declared it to be the "absolute antithesis of the West", the "bearer of the planetary mission of liberating the world from the 'shackles of capitalism'" (ibid.: 182–183, 185). The Third Rome was transformed for a while into the Third International, without, however, renouncing its mission as the *katechon*, as the restraining force against the empire of evil. For Maler, the "last stage" in the struggle against the Antichrist will be the "eschatological war of the Third Rome against the Third Carthage", the "Anglo-American Atlantic civilization" (ibid.: 177).

The formula of the Third Rome and the figure of the *katechon*, the restrainer of "global evil", have become trademarks of Russian anti-Westerners and conspiracy theorists and their shrill scenario of a global apocalyptic "final battle" against the New World Order (Morozova 2009; Engström 2014; Østbø 2016). Under the title *The Russian Doctrine. The State Ideology of Putin's Era*, a collective of national-patriotic authors – among them Arkadii Maler – published an ultra-conservative and anti-Western manifesto of over 1,000 pages in 2005 and 2006, which also found the support of high church dignitaries (*Russkaia doktrina* 2016). In their draft of an "organic ideological platform" for the future Russia, the authors deal in detail with the "historiosophical" idea of the Third Rome and its mission as a *katechon* against the "paganism" of the West (ibid.: 68–72, 116–120). They call for positive identification with Russia's history and its figures of light, Saint Serafim of Sarov, the "eschatological leader of the Russian people at the end of time", the Mother of God ("She Who Reigns"), and Stalin, who, like the Pauline *katechon*, fought "lawlessness" (*bezzakonie*) and laid the "foundation for a great future" (ibid.: 131–132, 153, 142–145).

Il'ia Glazunov: painted apocalypses

Both the Antichrist and the visible signs of his coming and rule are completely trivialized and turned into an item of spectacular marketing in the painted apocalypses of Il'ia Glazunov (1930–2017), former court painter of the Politburo and one of the most popular artists of post-Soviet Russia, while his critics call him *korol'kicha*, "the king of kitsch". His paintings on national and religious themes, displayed since 2004 in a special state-sponsored and pompously furnished museum in the centre of Moscow, feature "dark forces" identifiably associated with modern Western values and with "Judeo-Masonic Bolshevism", while Holy Russia and her last Emperor appear as victims of their conspiracy (Hagemeister 2004).

The monumental, often-reproduced painting *The Great Experiment* (1990)[23] shows eminent figures and events of twentieth-century Russian history, from the bright days of Tsarism to the dark reign of the Bolsheviks and the turmoil of *perestroika*. The centre of the painting is dominated by the red outlines of a five-pointed star or pentagram, according to Glazunov an "ancient cabalistic sign, symbol of evil" (Reznik 1996: 239). At the edge of the star one can recognize the Jewish murderer of Nicholas II and his family, Iakov (Iankel' Khaimovich) Iurovskii, drinking a blood-red liquid from a glass.[24] His victims are surrounded by a halo, a sea of flames blazing below them, in which a snake winds, dotted with five-pointed stars. St. George, patron saint of Moscow, pierces its head with a lance. In the centre of the red star, so to speak in the centre of evil, there is a smaller pentagram covered with cabalistic, alchemic and astrological signs and surrounded by the heads of leading Marxists and Bolsheviks of Jewish descent. It is the "Seal of the Antichrist". Glazunov reproduced this particular detail from the front page of an apocalyptic volume by Sergei Nilus, *Near Are the Coming Antichrist and the Kingdom of the Devil on Earth* (1911), which contains the *Protocols of the Elders of Zion*. This also enables the serpent on Glazunov's painting to be decoded: it is the "Symbolic Serpent" that appears and is described in the *Protocols*. The serpent represents the progress of the Jewish conspiracy. Starting from Jerusalem at the time of Solomon, the serpent's head moves through the European states until, with Zionist immigration, it returns to the point of its origin. The serpent signifies that the world is ruled from (and, literally, encircled by) Zion (De Michelis 1999). Glazunov's painting "exposes" those truly responsible for Russia's dismal fate and sufferings in the twentieth century; in other words, it serves the same purpose as the *Protocols*.

Glazunov himself appears in his own work as an apocalyptic visionary. For example, in his enigmatic *Mystery of the Twentieth Century* (1999)[25] the artist is depicted raising the curtain that used to disguise reality, thus allowing the observer to look deep into the *mirovaia zakulisa* (literally "global backstage"), the driving forces of world events. Glazunov also reveals his Manichean conspiracist worldview in his articles and interviews, though nowhere does it come across as clearly as in his autobiography *Russia Crucified* (2004–2008). There, the artist talks of history manipulated by a secret Satanic power (vol. 1, 2004: 13, 185, 262–266, 326), which in its pursuit of world domination makes use of the corroding effects of humanism, liberalism and democracy, consistently working towards the destruction of Russia and the "genocide of the Russian people" (vol. 2, 2008: 28).

Conclusion

The experience of multiple crises and the fear of catastrophe in post-Soviet Russia have created particularly favourable conditions for interpretations along the lines of salvation history. The "apocalyptic matrix", with its eschatologically defined figures of saviours and enemies, offers guidance, clear criteria for inclusion and exclusion, and ground for solidarization – all at the same time. The impenetrable patterns of ties and anonymous structures are vividly personified in tangible subjects of redemption and corruption. The "enemy" are the agents and beneficiaries of Western modernity, behind whom stands the well-disguised seductive Antichrist, to be exposed and vanquished. His antagonist in the cosmic struggle is Holy Russia, the eschatological Third Rome as the *katechon*, chosen and called to oppose the absolute Evil. From this way of seeing the world arises a sense of mission that makes up for the feeling of powerlessness, compensates for the supposed humiliation and fills all the suffering and sacrifice with a comprehensive, ultimate meaning.

Notes

1 Berdiaev's own interpretation of history is also eschatological. For him, the question concerning the meaning of history can only be answered from a final point: "How is it possible to understand the meaning of history without knowing what the last stage of history will be like? ... It is evident that a philosophy of history cannot be scientific; it can only be prophetic. It postulates the vision of a light that streams from the future; and it is only this light that proclaims a meaning for history. History has a meaning only if it is going to come to an end" (Berdyaev 1949: 168–169).

2 Eschatological currents were also widespread under Soviet rule, especially among the followers of the "True Orthodox Church", the so-called "Catacomb Church", but also among the numerous Christian sects; for some of them Lenin was the "Messiah of the twentieth century", for others the Antichrist. See, e.g., Agurskij (1988).

3 http://www.orthodox.net/articles/vision-of-st-john-of-kronstadt.html; accessed 17 March 2021.

4 The concept of "historiosophy" comes from August Cieszkowski (1814–1894), one of the founders of Polish messianism, who outlined an active teleology of history in his *Prolegomena to a Historiosophy* (1838). While in the West the word "metahistory" has since the publication of Hayden White's eponymous book in 1973 been taken to mean that writing a history is essentially a poetic act, in Russia the term has a completely different meaning. As early as in the beginning of the twentieth century the religious philosopher Sergei Bulgakov

(1871–1944) used it to designate "the object of the Apocalypse", namely the hidden "noumenal side of that universal process, the other aspect of which reveals itself to us as history" (1911: 103).

5 Usually, the following periods and events are mentioned as stations of Russia's Way of the Cross: the "Tatar yoke" when Russia drew the enemies of Christianity to itself and through its sacrifice, saved the Western civilization; then, the invasion of the Latin West in the early seventeenth century (the "Polish yoke") and finally, "the catastrophe of 1917".

6 Others, such as the nationalist publicist Valerii Khatiushin (1995), see in the collapse of the Soviet Union the work of the Antichrist (identified with Mikhail Gorbachev – "Mikhail the Marked"). The "Prince of Darkness" and his legions were preparing a five-year bloodbath in which Russia would be crucified; then she would be resurrected as leader of the world.

7 According to the so-called doctrine of substitution, after the "betrayal" of Israel (analogous to the apostasy of a part of the angels, who then became demons), her chosenness and her messianic mission were passed on to Holy Russia and her "God-bearing people"; the Orthodox Church became the "New Israel"; its holy sites the "New (or Second) Jerusalem". When Paul declared that in the end "all Israel will be saved" (*Rom* 11:26), he had in mind the Orthodox Church of Jesus Christ to which the Jews will have to convert (Nazarov 2005: 933–934, 945).

8 In Russian, the role of the "autocrat" (*samoderzhets*) as the *katechon* (*uderzhivaiushchii*) is apparent on the etymological level also; Russian *derzhat'* corresponds to the Greek *katéchein*. Just like the Antichrist and his agents, the mysterious figure of *to katéchon / ho katéchōn* (in Paul's epistle the word is first neuter and then masculine), which delays the Last Judgement and the coming of the Kingdom of God, has always lent itself to associations with ever changing images, groups or political powers. Thus Carl Schmitt (1888–1985), the "crown jurist" for the Third Reich and "apocalypticist of the counterrevolution" (Jacob Taubes), identified liberalism, Bolshevism, and Judaism with the Antichrist (or his agents) and recognized the *katechon* in Hitler's dictatorship. In 1947 he noted: "I believe in the *katechon*: it is for me the only way to understand and find meaning in history as a Christian" (Schmitt 2015: 47). Schmitt and his political theology are intensively received in Russian intellectual circles (cf. note. 20).

9 See Platonov (2001: 296–324); Fomin (2002b); Mul'tatuli (2010: 412–579). For a critical analysis, see Slater (2007: 71–78); Bagdasarian and Resnianskii (2018); Shtyrkov (2019). Orthodox nationalists and some Church officials also demanded to have Nicholas II and his family canonized as "martyred by the Jews". The demand, however, was declined by the leading officials of the Moscow Patriarchate (Khizhii 2014). In November 2017, the ritual murder allegation was raised again by Bishop Tikhon (Shevkunov), rumoured to be Putin's "spiritual advisor" (Taguieff 2020b: 52–55).

10 Fomin (2006: 351). Already in the early antibolshevik-antisemitic polemic, the fate of the last Tsar was compared to, or equated with, the Passion of Christ (Vinberg 1922; Khizhii 2014). Illustrative examples from a more recent time include the patriotic songs of the well-known singer Zhanna Bichevskaia or the films *The Atonement* (1992) and *The Russian Golgotha* (2000).

11 In the time of Peter the Great, there were rumours of the real Tsar having been exchanged for a Jew from the tribe of Dan, which made Peter into a "Jewish tsar anointed by the devil". For the Russian Old Believers who saw that the last

kingdom of true faith, the Third Rome, had collapsed, as well as for numerous sectarians, the autocracy and the succession of monarchs were an embodiment of the Antichrist. For more on the demonic conception of Russian rulers, see Platt (2000).

12 The birth date of the Antichrist, which was "calculated" by the famous swindler Léo Taxil over a century ago, can be explained through the magic of numbers: The sum of the digits composing 1962 is 18, thus 6 + 6 + 6, the number of the apocalyptic Beast. According to the Old Russian (Byzantine) calendar, 1992 is the year 7500 "since the creation of the world".

13 Jewish extremists are planning, indeed, to remove the Islamic sacred sites from Haram al-Sharif and to erect the Third Temple in their place; its model is already on display in Jerusalem's Old City. They are being supported by Christian Zionists who hope to accelerate the Second Coming (Gorenberg 2002).

14 Already in the mid-seventeenth century eschatologically inclined Old Believers, as well as supporters of apocalyptic sects, refused to accept documents issued by the state (passports, tax reports, edicts) as well as money, claiming that they bore "the seal of the Antichrist".

15 The Synod of the Bishops of the Moscow Patriarchate confirmed in March 2000 that the bar code included the number 666 and asked the authorities, in consideration of the believers in Russia, to change the bar code system to one deviating from the international standard.

16 The effect of such propaganda was apparent in April 1993, when three monks in the newly reopened monastery Optina Pustyn' were killed by a man who was, apparently, mentally disturbed. The extreme nationalist press, including the major Communist newspaper *Pravda*, appealed to the authority of Sergei Nilus as an "outstanding expert in Jewish symbolism, Zionism and Masonry", and thus interpreted the act as an attack by the Antichrist and as a Jewish (Hasidic) ritual murder commissioned by conspiratorial Satanic powers (Shumskii 1993; Gerasimov 1993; Korolev 1993; Tikhon 1993).

17 For all that, the enormous popularity of apocalyptic writings is not a specifically Russian phenomenon, as a comparison with the USA shows. With over 80 million copies sold and places on the *New York Times* bestseller list, the series of "Antichrist thrillers" by Tim LaHaye and Jerry B. Jenkins under the general title *Left Behind* (1995–2007) is probably the most successful product of modern apocalyptic mass narratives, also in commercial terms (Barkun 2003).

18 Since 1969, the Orthodox St. Herman of Alaska Brotherhood in Platina, CA, founded by Seraphim, has published Nilus's (carefully purged) works and posthumous materials.

19 The Russian translation of this book as well as the separately published chapter on UFOs (*NLO: Nepoznannye letaiushchie ob-ekty v svete pravoslavnoi vere*) became bestsellers in post-Soviet Russia (the Volgograd 1991 edition alone had a circulation of 75,000 copies).

20 The antagonism of land and sea, the categorical distinction between friend and foe, and the concept of the *katechon* go back to Carl Schmitt, as whose student Dugin describes himself.

21 This doctrine acquired popularity primarily through the controversial television documentary *The Fall of an Empire – the Lesson of Byzantium* (2008) by then Archimandrite Tikhon (Georgii Shevkunov). In the film, the fall of Byzantium exemplifies in an undisguised historical analogy the continuous threat to which

the Orthodox world is exposed because of a conspiracy of the Latin West (Hagemeister 2016: 15–20).

22 For the propagation of Russia's katechonic anti-Western mission, Maler founded the club "Katechon" in 1999 at the Institute of Philosophy of the Russian Academy of Sciences in Moscow. Since 2005, he has been publishing the almanac *Northern Katechon*. "Katechon" is also the name of a prominent think tank founded in 2015 by Konstantin Malofeev, an oligarch and advisor to Putin.

23 http://glazunov.ru/en/art/monumental-works/works/62-the-great-experiment; accessed 21 September 2021.

24 Glasunov also shows the allegedly cabalistic signs on the wall of the cellar room in the Ipat'ev house, which are supposed to prove the ritual character of the murder of the Tsar and his family by the Jewish agents of the Antichrist. Time and again, the painter has argued that the tragedy in Ekaterinburg was a "ritual murder", carried out on the orders of a "chosen minority". The antisemitic legend knows of yet another prominent "ritual murder victim" – the Tsarevich Dmitrii Ivanovich, who died mysteriously in Uglich in 1591. Glazunov did not miss the opportunity to portray the pale, exsanguinated boy with a gaping gash on his neck.

25 http://glazunov.ru/en/art/monumental-works/works/68-mystery-of-the-20th -century; accessed 21 September 2021.

Bibliography

Unpublished manuscripts

Cherikover, Il'ia (1934a), *Poslednie gody zhizni S.A. Nilusa (predvaritel'naia spravka)*, typoscript, not signed, not dated [1934], Stanford, Hoover Institution, The Boris I. Nicolaevsky Collection, series 11, box 20, folder 14.

——(1934b), *"Protokoly", ikh istochniki i ikh rasprostraniteli (obzor)*, typoscript, not dated [1934], Stanford, Hoover Institution, The Boris I. Nicolaevsky Collection, series 11, box 20, folder 3.

Nikolaevskii, Boris (s.d.), *O proiskhozhdenii "Protokolov sionskikh mudretsov"*, typoscript, The Boris I. Nicolaevsky Collection, Stanford, Hoover Institution, series 11, box 20, folder 5.

——Über die Entstehung der "Protokolle der Weisen von Zion". (Einführung), typoscript, AfZ: IB SIG Berner Prozess, boxes 55 and 84.

Nilus, Sergei Sergeevich (1936), *Au Service Mondial à Erfurt*, Grodzisk, 24 March 1936, typoscript, Sterling Memorial Library, Yale University, New Haven: Coll. 359, box 26.

Books and articles

Anon. (1877), "In the Toils. Mrs. Ralston's Strange Infatuation for a Dashing Adventurer", *San Francisco Chronicle*, 27 November, p. 3.

——(1889a), "A West End Libel Case: Remarkable Revelations", *The Manchester Guardian*, 11 October, p. 6.

——(1889b), "Letter from London", *The Japan Weekly Mail*, 30 November, pp. 505–506.

——(ca. 1890), Private Vigilance Society, *Concerning the man John Arthur Chandor, alias Count Chandor, alias Captain Chandor, alias Montagu Chandor, alias Captain Carlton, &c.*, s.l. [London].

——(1903), "Programa [sic] zavoevan'ia mira evreiami", *Znamia* 190 (28 August/10 September) – 200 (7/20 September).

——(1920), From a correspondent, "'The Jewish Peril.' A Disturbing Pamphlet: Call for Inquiry", *The Times*, 8 May, (available online: https://www.thetimes.co.uk/archive/article/1920-05-08/15/13.html, last accessed 21 September 2021).

——(1921a), "'Protocols Forged in Paris', Says Princess Radziwill in an Exclusive Interview with Isaac Landman", *American Hebrew and Jewish Messenger*, 25 February, p. 422.

——(1921b), "Nilus, Fanatic Author of 'Zion Protocols', Admitted in 1909 They Were Tissue of Lies", *New York Call*, 13 June, p. 6.

——(1921c), "Nilus, Perpetrator of the Protocols, Exposed. A.M. du Chayla, in 'La Tribune Juive', Explains How Protocols Came into the Possession of Nilus, His Fanatic Belief in Them and Their Origin", *American Hebrew and Jewish Messenger*, 17 June, pp. 119, 121, 128, 129, 136.

——(1933), *Confrontation der "Geheimnisse der Weisen von Zion" ("Die Zionistischen Protokolle") mit ihrer Quelle "Dialogue aux Enfers entre Machiavel et Montesquieu"*. *Der Nachweis der Fälschung*, Basel: Rechtsschutzabteilung des Schweizerischen Israelitischen Gemeindebundes.

——(1934), "Juristische Rundschau", *Deutsche Juristen-Zeitung* 39 (23), pp. 1461–1465.

——(1935a), "Novye dannye o 'Sionskikh protokolakh'. Zaiavlenie chikagskogo sviashch. G. Verkhovskogo", *Novoe russkoe slovo*, 2 January.

——(1935b), "Proof 'Protocols' Are False Given Chicago Paper by Russian Priest", *Jewish Daily Bulletin*, 3 January.

——(1935c), "Kniaginia Golitsyna", *Poslednie novosti*, 5133, 13 April, p. 4.

——(1937) [Elena Nilus-Ozerova], "Pis'mo s izvestiem o smerti S.A. Nilusa, 23 fevr. 1929 g.", in: *Plamennaia liubov'. Pamiati S. A. Nilusa*, New York: P. Georges, pp. 14–15.

——(1938), "Spionage und Judenhetze", *Israelitisches Wochenblatt für die Schweiz*, 11 November, p. 1.

——(1969) [Elena Kontsevich], "Sergei Aleksandrovich Nilus. Kratkoe zhizneopisanie avtora", in: *Sergei Nilus, Na beregu Bozh'ei reki. Chast' 2*, San Francisco: Orthodox Christian Books & Icons, pp. 1–42.

——(1972), *World Conquest Through World Government. The Protocols of the Learned Elders of Zion*, transl. from the Russian of Sergyei A. Nilus by Victor E. Marsden, 85th edn., Chulmleigh: Britons Publishing Co.

——(1994), "Arkhivnye dokumenty presledovaniia dukhovenstva chernigovskoi eparkhii v 1926–1936 gg.", *Pravoslavnaia zhizn'* 9, pp. 1–17.

——(1996), "'Tak istiazuetsia i raspinaetsia istina...' A. F. Losev v retsenziiakh OGPU", *Istochnik. Vestnik Arkhiva Prezidenta RF* 4, pp. 115–129.

Agurskij, Michail (1988), "L'aspect millénariste de la révolution bolchevique", *Cahiers du Monde russe et soviétique* 19, pp. 487–513.

Akhmetova, Mariia (2005), "Ozhidanie kontsa sveta v religioznykh subkul'turakh postsovetskoi Rossii," in: Eadem, ed., *Sovremennaia rossiiskaia mifologiia*, Moscow: RGGU, pp. 207–238.

——(2008), "Knowledge, Science, and the Scientist in Contemporary Mythology: A Study of Quasi-Scientific Narratives Collected from People Involved in Russian Religious Organizations", *Folklorica* 13, pp. 1–24.

——(2010), *Konets sveta v odnoi otdel'no vziatoi strane: Religioznye soobshchestva postsovetskoi Rossii i ikh èskhatologicheskii mif*, Moscow: OGI, RGGU.

Arendt, Hannah (1951), *The Origins of Totalitarianism*, New York: Harcourt, Brace & Co.

——(1986), *Elemente und Ursprünge totaler Herrschaft*, Munich: R. Piper.

Aronov, Lev (1991), "Primechaniia", in: Vladimir Burtsev, ed., *V pogone za provokatorami. "Protokoly sionskikh mudretsov"* – *dokazannyi podlog*, Moscow: Slovo, pp. 352–426.

Aronov, Lev, Khenrik [Henryk] Baran, and Dmitrii Zubarev (2006), K predystorii "Protokolov Sionskikh mudretsov". Iu. D. Glinka i ee pis'mo imperatoru Aleksandru III, *Novoe literaturnoe obozrenie* 82, pp. 169–182.

——(2009), "Kniaginia Ekaterina Radzivill i 'Protokoly sionskikh mudretsov'. Mistifikatsiia kak obraz zhizni", *Novoe literaturnoe obozrenie* 96, pp. 76–133.

——(2011), "Toward the prehistory of the Protocols. Iustin'ia Dmitrievna Glinka and her letter to Emperor Alexander III.", in: Esther Webman, ed., *The Global Impact of The Protocols of the Elders of Zion: A Century-Old Myth*, London and New York: Routledge, pp. 27–43.

Bagdasarian, Vardan (2006), "Apokalipsis – segodnia: ėskhatologicheskie poiski v sovremennoi Rossii", in: Dmitrii Andreev, Aleksandr Neklessa, and Vadim Prozorov, eds., *Ėskhatologicheskii sbornik*, Saint Petersburg: Aleteiia, pp. 435–453.

—— and Sergei Resnianskii (2018), "Versiia o 'ritual'nom ubiistve' tsarskoi sem'i v istoricheskoi literature i obshchestvennom diskurse", *Voprosy istorii* 3, pp. 35–48.

Bagdasarov, Roman and Sergei Fomin, eds., (1995), *Neizvestnyi Nilus*, 2 vols., Moscow: Pravoslavnyi palomnik.

Baigent, Michael, Richard Leigh, and Henry Lincoln (1990 [1982]), *The Holy Blood and the Holy Grail*, 16th edn., London: Corgi Books.

Baran, Henryk (2008), "O rannei publitsistike A.M. diu Shaila. Konteksty 'Protokolov Sionskikh mudretsov'", in: Ronald Vroon, ed., *I vremia i mesto: Istoriko-filologicheskii sbornik k shestidesiatiletiiu Aleksandra L'vovicha Ospovata*, Moscow: Novoe izdatel'stvo, pp. 454–467.

Barkun, Michael (2003), *A Culture of Conspiracy: Apocalyptic Visions in Contemporary America*, Berkeley: University of California Press.

Basin, Il'ia (1996), "Ėskhatologiia prepodobnogo Serafima Sarovskogo", *Khristianos* 5, pp. 89–104.

Battini, Michele (2010), *Socialism of Fools: Capitalism and Modern Anti-Semitism*, New York: Columbia University Press.

Beglov, Aleksei (2014), "Eschatological Expectations in Post-Soviet Russia: Historical Context and Modes of Interpretation", in: Katya Tolstaya, ed., *Orthodox Paradoxes. Heterogenities and Complexities in Contemporary Russian Orthodoxy*, Leiden and Boston: Brill, pp. 106–133.

Begunov, Iurii (1996), *Tainye sily v istorii Rossii. Sbornik statei i dokumentov*, 2nd edn., Saint Petersburg: Izd. im. A.S. Suvorina.

Beliaev, Aleksandr (1898), *O bezbozhii i Antikhriste*, vols. 1–2, Sergiev Posad: Tip. A.I. Snegirevoi; rpt. Moscow: Palomnik 1996.

Ben-Itto, Hadassa (1998), *"Die Protokolle der Weisen von Zion"* – *Anatomie einer Fälschung*, Berlin: Aufbau-Verlag.

———(2005), *The Lie That Wouldn't Die: The Protocols of the Elders of Zion*, London: Vallentine Mitchell.

Benz, Wolfgang (2020), *Vom Vorurteil zur Gewalt. Politische und soziale Feindbilder in Geschichte und Gegenwart*, Freiburg: Herder.

Berdiaev, Nikolai (1923), *Smysl istorii. Opyt filosofii chelovecheskoi sud'by*, Berlin: Obelisk.

Berdyaev, Nicolas (1947), *The Russian Idea*, London: Geoffrey Bles.

———(1949), *The Divine and the Human*, London: Geoffrey Bles.

Bergmeister, Karl (1937) (Hans Jonak von Freyenwald), *Der jüdische Weltverschwörungsplan. Die Protokolle der Weisen von Zion vor dem Strafgerichte in Bern*, Erfurt: U. Bodung.

Bernstein, Herman (1935), *The Truth about "The Protocols of Zion": A Complete Exposure*, New York: Covici Friede. New edn., New York: Ktav, 1971.

Bessonov, Igor (2014), *Russkaia narodnaia ėskhatologiia: istoriia i sovremennost'*, Moscow: Gnozis.

Bethea, David M. (1989), *The Shape of Apocalypse in Modern Russian Fiction*, Princeton, NJ: Princeton University Press.

Billington, James H. (1966), *The Icon and the Axe: An Interpretive History of Russian Culture*, New York: Alfred A. Knopf.

———(2004), *Russia in Search of Itself*, Washington, DC: Woodrow Wilson Center Press.

Blackstock, Paul W. (1966), *Agents of Deceit: Frauds, Forgeries and Political Intrigue Among Nations*, Chicago: Quadrangle Books.

Bondy, Louis W. (1946), *Racketeers of Hatred. Julius Streicher and the Jew-Baiter's International*, London: Newman Wolsey.

Borenstein, Eliot (2019), *Plots Against Russia: Conspiracy and Fantasy After Socialism*, Ithaca: Cornell University Press.

Brechtken, Magnus (1997), *"Madagaskar für die Juden." Antisemitische Idee und politische Praxis 1885–1945*, Munich: Oldenbourg.

Bronner, Stephen Eric (2019), *A Rumor about the Jews: Conspiracy, Anti-Semitism, and the Protocols of Zion*, 2nd edn., Cham: Palgrave Macmillan.

Budnitskii, Oleg (1999), *Evrei i russkaia revoliutsiia. Materialy i issledovaniia*, Moscow and Jerusalem: Gesharim.

Bulgakov, Sergei (1911), "Apokaliptika i sotsializm", in: idem, *Dva grada*, vol. 2, Moscow: Put', pp. 51–127.

Burtsev, Vladimir (1921), "Sionskie protokoly", *Obshchee delo* 273, 14 April, p. 2.

———(1938), *"Protokoly sionskikh mudretsov". Dokazannyi podlog (Rachkovskii sfabrikoval "Protokoly sionskikh mudretsov", a Gitler pridal im mirovuiu izvestnost'*, Paris: Oreste Zeluk.

Butmi, Georgii (1907), *Oblichitel'nye rechi. Vragi roda chelovecheskogo. Chetvertoe, obrabotannoe i dopolnennoe izdanie*, Saint Petersburg: Tip. Uchilishcha Gluchonemykh.

Bytwerk, Randall L. (2015), "Believing in 'Inner Truth': The Protocols of the Elders of Zion in Nazi Propaganda, 1933–1945", *Holocaust and Genocide Studies* 29, pp. 212–229.

Carlson, John Roy (Avedis Derounian) (1943), *Under Cover: My Four Years in the Nazi Underworld of America – The Amazing Revelation of How Axis Agents and Our Enemies Within Are Now Plotting to Destroy the United States*, New York: E.P. Dutton.

Chavchavadze, David (1990), *Crowns and Trenchcoats. A Russian Prince in the CIA*, New York: Atlantic Internat. Publ.

Clay, J. Eugene (1998), "Apocalypticism in Eastern Europe", in: Stephen J. Stein, ed., *The Encyclopedia of Apocalypticism*, vol. 3, New York: Continuum, pp. 293–321.

Clover, Charles (2017), *Black Wind, White Snow: The Rise of Russia's New Nationalism*, New Haven and London: Yale University Press.

Cohn, Norman (1996 [1967]), *Warrant for Genocide: The Myth of the Jewish World-Conspiracy and the Protocols of the Elders of Zion*, London: Serif.

Comnène Paléologue, Prince I. (1965), *Ordem Imperial Constantiniana Militar de São Jorge*, Rio de Janeiro.

Coogan, Kevin (1999), *Dreamer of the Day: Francis Parker Yockey and the Postwar Fascist International*, Brooklyn, NY: Autonomedia.

——(2021), *The Spy Who Would be Tsar: The Mystery of Michal Goleniewski and the Far-Right Underground*, London and New York: Routledge.

Curtiss, John S. (1942), *An Appraisal of the Protocols of the Elders of Zion*, New York: Columbia University Press.

Damascene (John Christensen) (1993), *Not of this World. The Life and Teachings of Fr. Seraphim Rose*, Forestville, CA: Fr. Seraphim Rose Foundation.

De Michelis, Cesare G. (1996), "Il principe N.D. Ževaxov e i 'Protocolli dei savi di Sion' in Italia", *Studi storici* 37 (3), pp. 747–770.

——(1997), "Machiavellismo e antimachiavellismo nei 'Protocolli dei savi di Sion'", *Magisterium* I, pp. 643–655.

——(1998), *Il manoscritto inesistente. I "Protocolli dei savi di Sion": un apocrifo del XX secolo*, Venezia: Marsilio.

——(1999), "Ot Ierusalima do Ierusalima. (Tsikl 'Simvolicheskogo Zmiia' v 'Protokolakh Sionskikh mudretsov')", in: Wolf Moskovich et al., eds., *Oh, Jerusalem!*, Pisa: Unversità degli Studi di Pisa, pp. 161–172.

——(2004), *The Non-Existent Manuscript: A Study of the* Protocols of the Sages of Zion, trans. from the Italian by Richard Newhouse, Lincoln and London: University of Nebraska Press.

——(2005), "Kniaz' N.D. Zhevakov i Italiia. (K istorii publikatsii v Italii 'Protokolov sionskikh mudretsov')", in: Wolf Moskovich and Svetlina Nikolova, eds., *Judaeo-Bulgarica, Judaeo-Russica et Palaeoslavica*, Jerusalem and Sofia: Hebrew University of Jerusalem, Bulgarian Academy of Sciences, pp. 231–251.

——(2009), "Un testimone 'perduto' dei *Protocolli*", *Russica Romana* 16, pp. 89–94.

Drault, Jean (1921), "Alexandre Dumas père et les 'Protocols'", *La Vieille France* 242 (15–21 September), pp. 21–32; 243 (22–29 September), pp. 22–32; 244 (30 September – 7 October), pp. 22–32.

Du Chayla, Alexandre (1913), "A propos du Procès de Kieff", *Revue contemporaine* 5/18 October, pp. 217–218.

——(1921a), "S.A. Nilus i 'Sionskie Protokoly'", *Poslednie novosti*, 12 May, pp. 2–3; 13 May, pp. 2–3.

——(1921b), "Vospominaniia o S.A. Niluse i Sionskikh Protokolakh. (1909–1920)", *Evreiskaia tribuna*, 14 May, pp. 1–7.

——(1921c), "Serge Alexandrovitch Nilus et les 'Protocoles des Sages de Sion' (1909–1920)", *La Tribune Juive* 72, 14 May, pp. 1–7.

Dudakov, Savelii (1993), *Istoriia odnogo mifa. Ocherki russkoi literatury XIX–XX vv.*, Moscow: Nauka.

Dugin, Aleksandr (1996), "Krestovyi pokhod solntsa", *Milyi angel* 2, pp. 52–80.

——(1997), "Katekhon i revoliutsiia", in: idem, *Tampliery proletariata. Natsional-bol'shevizm i initsiaciia*, Moscow: Arktogeia, pp. 52–59.

——(1999), *Absoliutnaia Rodina. Puti Absoliuta. Metafizika Blagoi Vesti. Misterii Evrazii*, Moscow: Arktogeia-tsentr.

——(2005), *Konspirologiia. Nauka o zagovorakh, sekretnykh obshchestvakh i tainoi voine*, Moscow: Evraziia.

Duncan, Peter J. S. (2000), *Russian Messianism: Third Rome, Revolution, Communism, and After*, London and New York: Routledge.

Eco, Umberto (1990), *The Limits of Interpretation*, Bloomington: Indiana University Press.

——(1994), *Six Walks in the Fictional Woods*, Cambridge, MA: Harvard University Press.

——(1998), *Serendipities: Language and Lunacy*, San Diego, New York, and London: Harcourt Brace & Co.

Eisner, Will (2005), *The Plot: The Secret Story of the Protocols of the Elders of Zion*, New York: Norton.

Ellis, Bill (2005), *The Protocols of the Learned Elders of Zion: The French Contribution to Transnational Conspiracy Theories*. Draft for Presentation at the 2005 American Folklore Society Annual Meeting, Atlanta, Georgia, https://www.academia.edu/29015136/The_Protocols_of_the_Learned_Elders_of_Zion_The_French_Contribution_to_Transnational_Conspiracy_Theories, last accessed 21 September 2021.

Engels, Friedrich (1888), *Ludwig Feuerbach und der Ausgang der klassischen deutschen Philosophie*, Stuttgart: J.H.W. Dietz.

Engström, Maria (2014), "Contemporary Russian Messianism and New Russian Foreign Policy", *Contemporary Security Policy* 3, pp. 356–379.

Èskhatologicheskii sbornik (2006), Dmitrii Andreev et al., eds., Saint Petersburg: Aleteiia.

Evans, Richard J. (2020), "Were the Protocols a 'warrant for genocide'?", in: idem, *The Hitler Conspiracies: The Third Reich and the Paranoid Imagination*, London: Allen Lane, pp. 13–45.

Evola, Julius (1937), "Studi sui 'Protocolli' ebraici. Trasformazioni del 'Regnum'", *La Vita Italiana* 25, pp. 535–544.

Fischer, Ben B. (1997), *Okhrana. The Paris Operations of the Russian Imperial Police*, Washington, DC: Central Intelligence Agency.

Flämming, Knud (1921), "Unterm Scheinwerfer. Der Verfasser der: Protokolle der Weisen von Zion" *Völkischer Beobachter* 39 (19 May), p. 3.

Fleischhauer, Ulrich (1935), *Die echten Protokolle der Weisen von Zion: Sachverständigengutachten, erstattet im Auftrage des Richteramtes V in Bern*, Erfurt: U. Bodung.

Fomin, Sergei (1993), "Vokrug altaria satany", *Veche* 43, pp. 55–71.

——(2002a), "Tretii Khram protiv Tret'ego Rima", *Russkii vestnik*, 22 July, p. 1.

——(2002b), "Ekaterinburgskoe ritual'noe ubiistvo", in: ... *I dany budut zhene dva kryla. Sbornik k 50-letiiu Sergeia Fomina*, Moscow: Palomnik, pp. 334–357.

——(2006), "'Tsar' v sakkose'. (K vosstanovleniiu Simfonii v Rossii)", in: Dmitrii Andreev, Aleksandr Neklessa, and Vadim Prozorov, eds., *Èskhatologicheskii sbornik*, Saint Petersburg: Aleteiia, pp. 317–357.

Fomin, Sergei and Tat'iana Fomina eds. (1998). *Rossiia pered vtorym prishestviem. Materialy k ocherku Russkoi èskhatologii*, 3rd edn., vols. 1–2, Moscow and Saint Petersburg: Obshchestvo sviatitelia Vasiliia Velikogo.

Fritsch, Theodor (1932), "Schlusswort", in: *Die Zionistischen Protokolle. Das Programm der internationalen Geheimregierung*, 11th edn., Leipzig: Hammer-Verlag, pp. 67–79.

Fry, L(eslie) (1921a), "Les 'Protocols' des Sages de Sion et l'Indépendance Américaine", *Revue Internationale des Sociétés Secrètes* 10 (3), pp. 293–302.

——(1921b), "Sur l'authenticité des Protocols. Achad ha-Am et le Sionisme", *La Vieille France* 218 (31 March–6 April), pp. 1–11.

——(1921c), *L'auteur des Protocols Achad ha-Am et le Sionisme*, Paris: Editions de La Vieille-France, 1921.

——(1921d), *Akhad-Kham (Asher Gintsberg). Tainyi vozhd' iudeiskii. (Perevod s frantsuzskogo)*, Berlin: Presse.

——(1923), *Achad Cham (Ascher Hinzberg). Der geheime Führer der Juden. Übersetzung aus dem Französischen und nach dem aus dem* [sic] *Russischen*, Munich: Oldenbourg.

——(1931a), *Waters Flowing Eastward*, Paris: R.I.S.S.

——(1931b), *Le retour des flots vers l'Orient. Le Juif, notre maître*, Chatou: British American Press.

——(1931c), "Les Missionnaires du Gnosticisme", *Revue Internationale des Sociétés Secrètes* 20, pp. 461–488.

——(1934a), *Waters Flowing Eastward*, 3rd edn., revised and enlarged, Chatou: British American Press.

——(1934b), *Léo Taxil et la Franc-Maçonnerie. Lettres inédites publiées par les amis de Monseigneur Jouin*, Chatou: British American Press.

——(1958), *Interfaith, World Government and Universal Religion*, s.l.

Fry, Michael (1934), *Hitler's Wonderland*, London: John Murray.

Fuller Robert, C. (1995), *Naming the Antichrist: The History of an American Obsession*, New York: Oxford University Press.

Garrard, John and Carol Garrard (2008), *Russian Orthodoxy Resurgent: Faith and Power in the New Russia*, Princeton and Oxford: Princeton University Press.

Gavriushin, Nikolai (1991), "Znameniia prishestviia Antikhristova", *Sovetskaia literatura* 1, pp. 155–158.

Gerasimov, Dmitrii (1993), "Sataninskoe plemia. Kto stoit za ubiitsei inokov?", *Pravda* 85 (5 May), p. 4.

Ginzburg, Carlo (2012), "Representing the Enemy: On the French Prehistory of the *Protocols*", in: idem, *Threads and Traces: True False Fictive*, Berkeley: University of California Press, pp. 151–164.

Glaser, Jennifer (2014), "Of Superheroes and Synecdoche: Holocaust Exceptionalism, Race, and the Rhetoric of Jewishness in America", in: Michael Bernard-Donals and Janice W. Fernheimer, eds., *Jewish Rhetorics: History, Theory, Practice*, Waltham, MA: Brandeis University Press, pp. 231–248.

Glazunov, Il'ia (1994), *Panorama*, August 31, p. 20.

——(2004–2008), *Rossiia raspiataia*, 4 vols. Moscow: Golos-Press.

Gorenberg, Gershom (2002), *The End of Days: Fundamentalism and the Struggle for the Temple Mount*, Oxford: Oxford University Press.

Graves, Philip (1921), *The Truth About "The Protocols". A Literary Forgery. From The Times of August 16, 17, and 18, 1921*, London: The Times.

Hachmeister, Lutz (1998), *Der Gegnerforscher: Die Karriere des SS-Führers Franz Alfred Six*, Munich: Beck.

Hagemeister, Michael (1991), "Wer war Sergej Nilus? (Versuch einer bio-bibliographischen Skizze)", *Ostkirchliche Studien* 40 (1), pp. 49–63; French transl. "Qui était Serguei Nilus?", *Politica Hermetica* 9, 1995, pp. 141–158.

——(1998), "Eine Apokalypse unserer Zeit. – Die Prophezeiungen des heiligen Serafim von Sarov über das Kommen des Antichrist und das Ende der Welt", in: Joachim Hösler and Wolfgang Kessler, eds., *Finis mundi – Endzeiten und Weltenden im östlichen Europa. Festschrift für Hans Lemberg zum 65. Geburtstag*, Stuttgart: Steiner, pp. 41–60.

——(2000), "Vladimir Solov'ev and Sergej Nilus: Apocalypticism and Judeophobia", in: Wil van den Bercken et al., eds., *Vladimir Solov'ev: Reconciler and Polemicist. Selected Papers of the International Vladimir Solov'ev Conference held at the University of Nijmegen, the Netherlands, in September 1998*, Leuven: Peeters, pp. 287–296.

——(2001), "Wiederverzauberung der Welt – Pavel Florenskijs Neues Mittelalter", in: Norbert Franz et al., eds., *Pavel Florenskij – Tradition und Moderne. Beiträge zum Internationalen Symposium an der Universität Potsdam, 5. bis 9. April 2000*, Frankfurt am Main: Peter Lang, pp. 21–41.

——(2002), "Die Protokolle der Weisen von Zion – eine Anti-Utopie oder der Große Plan in der Geschichte?", in: Helmut Reinalter, ed., *Verschwörungstheorien. Theorie –Geschichte – Wirkung*, Innsbruck: Studien Verlag, pp. 45–57.

——(2003), "Nilus, Sergej Aleksandrovič", in: *Biographisch-Bibliographisches Kirchenlexikon*, vol. 21, Nordhausen: Bautz, pp. 1063–1067.

——(2004), "Anti-Semitism, Occultism, and Theories of Conspiracy in Contemporary Russia – The Case of Ilya Glazunov", in: Vladimir Paperni and Wolf Moskovich, eds., *Anti-Semitism and Philo-Semitism in the Slavic World and Western Europe*, Haifa & Jerusalem: University of Haifa & Hebrew University of Jerusalem, pp. 235–241.

——(2005a), "Predki i rodstvenniki Sergeia Aleksandrovicha Nilusa", in: Sergei Nilus: *Polnoe sobranie sochinenii v shesti tomakh*, vol. 6, Moscow: Obshchestvo sviatitelia Vasiliia Velikogo, pp. 242–259.

——(2005b), "Nilus, Sergej", in: Richard E. Levy, ed., *Antisemitism. A Historical Encyclopedia of Prejudice and Persecution*, vol. 2, Santa Barbara, CA.: ABC-Clio, pp. 508–510.

——(2006), "The *Protocols of the Elders of Zion* and the Myth of a Jewish Conspiracy in Post-Soviet Russia", in: Jan Herman Brinks et al., eds., *Nationalist Myths and Modern Media: Contested Identities in the Age of Globalization*, London and New York: Tauris, pp. 243–255.

——(2008a), "The *Protocols of the Elders of Zion*: Between History and Fiction", *New German Critique* 35 (1), pp. 83–95.

——(2008b), "Jonak von Freyenwald, Hans", in: Wolfgang Benz, ed., *Handbuch des Antisemitismus. Judenfeindschaft in Geschichte und Gegenwart*, 2/1, Berlin: de Gruyter, pp. 411–412.

——(2008c), "Kruschewan, Pawel", in: Wolfgang Benz, ed., *Handbuch des Antisemitismus. Judenfeindschaft in Geschichte und Gegenwart*, 2/1, Berlin: de Gruyter, pp. 441–442.

——(2009a), "V poiskakh svidetel'stv o proiskhozhdenii 'Protokolov sionskikh mudretsov': Izdanie, ischeznuvshee iz Leninskoi biblioteki", *Novoe literaturnoe obozrenie* 96, pp. 134–153.

——(2009b), "Butmi de Kazman, Georgi", in: Wolfgang Benz, ed., *Handbuch des Antisemitismus. Judenfeindschaft in Geschichte und Gegenwart*, 2/1, Berlin: de Gruyter, pp. 117–118.

——(2010), "Trilogie der Apokalypse – Vladimir Solov'ev, Serafim von Sarov und Sergej Nilus über das Kommen des Antichrist und das Ende der Weltgeschichte", in: Wolfram Brandes and Felicitas Schmieder, eds., *Antichrist. Konstruktionen von Feindbildern*, Berlin: Akademie Verlag, pp. 255–275.

——(2011a), "Das Dritte Rom gegen den Dritten Tempel – Der Antichrist im postsowjetischen Russland", in: Mariano Delgado and Volker Leppin, eds., *Der Antichrist. Zur Wirkungsgeschichte eines apokalyptischen Motivs in Judentum, Christentum und Islam*, Fribourg: Academic Press & Stuttgart: Kohlhammer, pp. 461–485.

——(2011b), "The Protocols of the Elders of Zion in Court. The Bern Trials, 1933–1937", in: Esther Webman, ed., *The Global Impact of The Protocols of the Elders of Zion: A century-old myth*, London and New York: Routledge, pp. 241–253.

——(2012a), "'Alles nur Betrug und Lüge'? Fakten und Fiktionen im Leben der Catherine Radziwill", in: Agnieszka Brockmann et al., eds., *Kulturelle Grenzgänge. Festschrift für Christa Ebert zum 65. Geburtstag*, Berlin: Frank & Timme, pp. 287–298.

——(2012b), "'The Antichrist as an Imminent Political Possibility.' Sergei Nilus and the Apocalyptical Reading of The Protocols of the Elders of Zion", in: Richard Landes and Steven T. Katz, eds., *The Paranoid Apocalypse: A Hundred-Year Retrospective on 'The Protocols of the Elders of Zion'*, New York: New York University Press, pp. 79–91.

——(2012c), "Zur Frühgeschichte der Protokolle der Weisen von Zion I: Im Reich der Legenden", in: Eva Horn and Michael Hagemeister, eds., *Die Fiktion von der jüdischen Weltverschwörung. Zu Text und Kontext der "Protokolle der Weisen von Zion"*, Göttingen: Wallstein, pp. 140–160.

——(2012d), "Zur Frühgeschichte der Protokolle der Weisen von Zion II: Das verschollene Exemplar der Lenin-Bibliothek", in: Eva Horn and Michael Hagemeister, eds., *Die Fiktion von der jüdischen Weltverschwörung. Zu Text und Kontext der "Protokolle der Weisen von Zion"*, Göttingen: Wallstein, pp. 161–189.

——(2013), "Carl Albert Loosli und der Berner Prozess um die *Protokolle der Weisen von Zion*", in: Gregor Spuhler, ed., *Anstaltsfeind und Judenfreund. Carl Albert Looslis Einsatz für die Würde des Menschen*. Zurich: Chronos, pp. 95–115.

——(2014), "The American Connection. Leslie Fry and the *Protocols of the Elders of Zion*", in: Marina Ciccarini, Nicoletta Marcialis, and Giorgio Ziffer, eds., *Kesarevo Kesarju. Scritti in onore di Cesare G. De Michelis*, Florence: Firenze University Press, pp. 217–228.

——(2015a), "The Protocols of the Elders of Zion – a Forgery?", in: Gabriella Catalano et al., eds., *La verità del falso: Studi in onore di Cesare G. De Michelis*, Rome: Viella, pp. 163–171.

——(2015b), "'Geheimnisse des Judentums' und ihre 'Enthüllungen'. Von *Biarritz zu den Protokollen der Weisen von Zion*", in: Philipp Mettauer and Barbara Staudinger, eds., *"Ostjuden" – Geschichte und Mythos*, Innsbruck: Studien Verlag, pp. 173–191.

——(2016), "'Bereit für die Endzeit.' Neobyzantismus in Russland", *Osteuropa* 11–12, pp. 15–42.

——(2017), *Die "Protokolle der Weisen von Zion" vor Gericht. Der Berner Prozess 1933–1937 und die "antisemitische Internationale"*, Zurich: Chronos.

——(2018), "The Third Rome against the Third Temple: Apocalypticism and Conspiracism in Post-Soviet Russia", in: Asbjørn Dyrendal et al., eds., *Handbook of Conspiracy Theory and Contemporary Religion*, Leiden: Brill, pp. 423–442.

—— and Torsten Metelka, eds., (2001), *Appendix 2. Materialien zu Pavel Florenskij*, Berlin: Kontext Verlag.

Hanebrink, Paul (2018), *A Specter Haunting Europe: The Myth of Judeo-Bolshevism*, Cambridge, MA, and London: Harvard University Press.

Hapgood, Norman (1922), "The Inside Story of Henry Ford's Jew-Mania. Henry Swallows Old Bait", *Hearst's International*, September, pp. 45–48, 133–134.

Heiber, Helmut (1966), *Walter Frank und sein Reichsinstitut für Geschichte des neuen Deutschlands*, Stuttgart: Deutsche Verlags-Anstalt.

Heiden, Konrad (1944), *The Fuehrer: Hitler's Rise to Power*, Boston: Houghton Mifflin.

Heil, Johannes (2006), *"Gottesfeinde" – "Menschenfeinde". Die Vorstellung von jüdischer Weltverschwörung (13. bis 16. Jahrhundert)*, Essen: Klartext-Verlag.

Heilbut, Iwan (1937), *Les vrais Sages de Sion*, Paris: Denoël.

Hillis, Faith (2017), "The 'Franco-Russian Marseillaise': International Exchange and the Making of Antiliberal Politics in Fin de Siècle France", *The Journal of Modern History* 89, pp. 39–78.

Hofer, Sibylle (2011a), "Verkannte Recht-Sprechung. Die Berner Prozesse um die 'Protokolle der Weisen von Zion' 1933–1937", *Zeitschrift für Neuere Rechtsgeschichte* 33 (1/2), pp. 25–41.

——(2011b), *Richter zwischen den Fronten. Die Urteile des Berner Prozesses um die "Protokolle der Weisen von Zion" 1933–1937*, Basel: Helbing & Lichtenhahn.

Horn, Eva (2012), "Das Gespenst der Arcana. Verschwörungsfiktion und Textstruktur der 'Protokolle der Weisen von Zion'", in: eadem and Michael Hagemeister, eds., *Die Fiktion von der jüdischen Weltverschwörung. Zu Text und Kontext der "Protokolle der Weisen von Zion"*, Göttingen: Wallstein, pp. 1–25.

Horowitz, Brian (2017), *The Russian-Jewish Tradition: Intellectuals, Historians, Revolutionaries*, Boston: Academic Studies Press.

Hosking, Geoffrey (1997), *Russia: People and Empire, 1592–1917*, Cambridge, MA: Harvard University Press.

Introvigne, Massimo (1994a), "Che cos'è la massoneria: il problema delle origini e le origini del problema", in: idem, ed., *Massoneria e religioni*, Torino: Elle Di Ci, pp. 13–62.

——(1994b), *Indagine sul satanismo. Satanisti e anti-satanisti dal Seicento ai nostri giorni*, Milano: Mondadori.

——(2005), *Gli Illuminati e il Priorato di Sion. La verità sulle due società segrete del Codice da Vinci e di Angeli e demoni*, Casale Monferrato: Piemme.

Ioann (Ivan Snychev) (1993a), "Bitva za Rossiiu", *Sovetskaia Rossiia* 21 (20 February), 1, p. 4.

——(1993b), "Pravoslavnaia revoliutsiia protiv sovremennogo mira", *Èlementy* 4, pp. 18–19.

——(1994), *Samoderzhavie dukha. Ocherki russkogo samosoznaniia*, Saint Petersburg: Izd. L. S. Iakovlevoi.

Isupov, Konstantin, ed., (1995), *Antikhrist. Iz istorii otechestvennoi dukhovnosti*, Moscow: Vysshaia shkola.

Iudin, Aleksei (2002), "Verkhovskii, Gleb Evgen'evich", in: *Katolicheskaia èntsiklopediia*, vol. 1: A–Z, Moscow: Izdat. Frantsiskantsev, p. 948.

Jeansonne, Glen (1996), *Women of the Far Right: The Mother's Movement and World War II.*, Chicago: University of Chicago Press.

Jonak von Freyenwald, Hans (1939), *Der Berner Prozeß um die Protokolle der Weisen von Zion. Akten und Gutachten, vol. 1: Anklage und Zeugenaussagen*, Erfurt: Bodung.

Jouin, Ernest (1922), *Le Péril Judéo-maçonnique, vol. 4: Les "Protocols" de 1901 de G. Butmi*, Paris: Revue Internationale des Sociétés Secrètes et Librairie Émile-Paul.

Kartashëv, Anton (1923), "Predislovie", in: Iurii Delevskii, ed., *Protokoly Sionskikh Mudretsov. Istoriia odnogo podloga*, Berlin: Èpokha, p. 8.

Kartsov, Iurii (1981), "Khronika raspada", *Novyi zhurnal* 144, pp. 95–132.

Kasper-Marienberg (2012), "Die 'Protokolle der Weisen von Zion' als klassische Utopie? Eine rhetorische Textanalyse", in: Eva Horn and Michael Hagemeister, eds., *Die Fiktion von der jüdischen Weltverschwörung. Zu Text und Kontext der "Protokolle der Weisen von Zion"*, Göttingen: Wallstein, pp. 26–50.

Katasonov, Valentin (2020), *Koronavirus. Ot virusa k diktature*, Moscow: Knizhnyi mir.

Katsis, Leonid (2000), *Russkaia eskhatologiia i russkaia literatura*, Moscow: OGI.

Katz, Steven T. (2001), *Continuity and Discontinuity between Christian and Nazi Antisemitism*, Tübingen: Mohr Siebeck.

Kellogg, Michael (2005), *The Russian Roots of Nazism: White Émigrés and the Making of National-Socialism 1917–1945*, Cambridge and New York: Cambridge University Press.

Khatiushin, Valerii (1995), "Esli poimen – spasemsia", *Molodaia gvardiia* 3, pp. 2–40.

Khizhii, Maksim (2014), "Kanonizatsiia Nikolaia II i ego sem'i: Offitsial'naia pozitsiia RPTs protiv antisemitizma pravykh radikalov", in: Viktoriia Mochalova, ed., *Materialy XXI Mezhdunarodnoi ezhegodnoi konferentsii po iudaike*, Moscow: Institut Slavianovedeniia RAN, pp. 236–442.

Kiš, Danilo (1990), "The Book of Kings and Fools", in: idem: *The Encycopedia of the Dead*, London: Faber and Faber.

Klier, John D. (1995), *Imperial Russia's Jewish Question 1855–1881*, Cambridge: Cambridge University Press.

——(1998), "The Dog That Didn't Bark: Anti-Semitism in Post-Communist Russia", in: Geoffrey Hosking and Robert Service, eds., *Russian Nationalism Past and Present*, Basingstoke: Macmillan.

Korolev, Aleksandr (1993), "'Brat Satany'. Ritual'noe ubiistvo monakhov v Optinoi Pustyni", *Trud* (5 May), p. 4.

Kozlov, Maksim (1990), "Besy i NLO", *Literaturnyi Irkutsk* 8, pp. 12–13.

Krushevan, Pavel (1903), (Foreword to) "Programa zavoevan'ia mira evreiami", *Znamia* 190 (28 August/10 September), p. 2.

Lavine, Harold (1940), *Fifth Column in America*, New York: Doubleday.

Levin, Nora (1968), *The Holocaust. The Destruction of European Jewry 1933–1945*, New York: Company.

Levkievskaia, Elena (2005), "Russkaia ideia v kontekste istoricheskikh mifologicheskikh modelei i mekhanizmy ikh obrazovaniia", in: Mariia Akhmetova, ed., *Sovremennaia rossiiskaia mifologiia*, Moscow: RGGU, pp. 175–206.

Levy, Richard S. (2014), "Setting the Record Straight Regarding 'The Protocols of the Elders of Zion': A Fool's Errand?", in: William C. Donahue and Martha B. Helfer, eds., *Nexus. Essays in German Jewish Studies 2*, Rochester: Camden House, pp. 43–61.

Livers, Keith A. (2020), *Conspiracy Culture: Post-Soviet Paranoia and the Russian Imagination*, Toronto: University of Toronto Press.

Livingston, Sigmund (1944), *Must Men Hate?*, Cleveland, Ohio: Crane Press.

Löwe, Heinz-Dietrich (1993), *The Tsars and the Jews: Reform, Reaction and Anti-Semitism in Imperial Russia, 1772–1917*, Chur: Harwood Academic Publ.

Longerich, Peter (2021), *Antisemitismus. Eine deutsche Geschichte. Von der Aufklärung bis heute*, Munich: Siedler Verlag.

Lotman, Iurii and Boris Uspenskii (1984), "The role of dual models in the dynamics of Russian culture", in: idem, *The Semiotics of Russian Culture*, ed. Ann Shukman, Ann Arbor: University of Michigan, pp. 3–35.

Lüthi, Urs (1992), *Der Mythos von der Weltverschwörung. Die Hetze der Schweizer Frontisten gegen Juden und Freimaurer – am Beispiel des Berner Prozesses um die "Protokolle der Weisen von Zion"*, Basel and Frankfurt am Main: Helbing & Lichtenhahn.

Maler, Arkadii (2005), *Dukhovnaia missiia Tret'ego Rima*, Moscow: Veche.

——(2007), "Neovizantizm kak novyi bol'shoi stil'", in: Aleksei Nilogov, ed., *Kto segodnia delaet filosofiiu v Rossii*, Moscow: Pokolenie, pp. 110–124.

Maurois, André (1981), *Prometheus oder Das Leben Balzacs*, Berlin and Weimar: Aufbau-Verlag.

Men'shikov, Mikhail (1902), "Zagovory protiv chelovechestva", in: idem, *Pis'ma k blizhnim*, Saint Petersburg: Izd. M.O. Men'shikova, pp. 222–226; also in: idem, *Pis'ma k blizhnim 1902*, Saint Petersburg: Mashina vremenii, 2019, pp. 286–302.

Mikhailovskii, Dmitrii (2000), "Tri Paskhi ispovednika. K biografii S.A. Nilusa", *Pravoslavnaia Rus'* 8, pp. 7–10.

Mitrokhin, Nikolai (2007), "Infrastruktura podderzhki pravoslavnoi èskhatologii v sovremennoi RPTs. Istoriia i sovremennost'", in: Marlène Laruelle, ed., *Russkii natsionalizm v politicheskom prostranstve*, Moscow: Franko-Rossiiskii tsentr gumanitarnykh i obshchestvennykh nauk, pp. 200–254.

Mjør, Kåre Johan (2020), "An eternal Russia: Oleg Platonov, the Institute for Russian Civilization and the nationalization of Russian thought", in: idem and Sanna Turoma, eds., *Russia as Civilization: ideological Discourses in Politics, Media, and Academia*, London and New York: Routledge, pp. 186–205.

Molchanov, Boris (1938), *"Taina bezzakoniia" i antikhrist*, s.l. (Harbin).

—— (1990), "Antikhrist", *Sankt-Peterburgskie eparkhial'nye vedomosti* 1, pp. 21–26.

Morcos, Saad (1961), *Juliette Adam*, Cairo: Dar al-Maaref.

Morozova, Galina (2009), *Tretii Rim protiv novogo mirovogo poriadka*, Moscow: Institut russkoi tsivilizatsii.

Mul'tatuli, Pëtr (2010), *Nikolai II. Doroga na Golgofu*, Moscow: Astrel'.

Nazarov, Mikhail (2005), *Vozhdiu Tret'ego Rima. K poznaniiu russkoi idei v apokalipsicheskoe vremia*, Moscow: Russkaia ideia.

Nilus, Sergei (1905), *Velikoe v malom i antikhrist, kak blizkaia politicheskaia vozmozhnost'. Zapiski pravoslavnogo*, Tsarskoe Selo: Tip. Tsarskosel'skogo Komiteta Krasnogo Kresta.

——(1909), *Dlia chego i komu nuzhny pravoslavnye monastyri*, Sergiev Posad: Tip. Sv.-Tr. Sergievoi Lavry.

——(1911), *Bliz griadushchii antikhrist i tsarstvo diavola na zemle*, Sergiev Posad: Tip. Sv.-Tr. Sergievoi Lavry.

——(1917), *"Bliz est', pri dverekh". O tom, chemu ne zhelaiut verit' i chto tak blizko. 4-e izdanie knigi "Bliz griadushchii antikhrist i tsarstvo diavola na zemle", pererabotannoe i znachitel'no dopolnennoe pozdneishimi issledovaniiami i nabliudeniiami*, Sergiev Posad: Tip. Sv.-Tr. Sergievoi Lavry.

——(1999–2005), *Polnoe sobranie sochinenii v shesti tomakh*, ed. Aleksandr Strizhev, 6 vols. Moscow: Obshchestvo sviatitelia Vasiliia Velikogo.

Nikolaevskii, Boris (1935), "Der neuzeitliche Antisemitismus und die 'Protokolle der Weisen von Zion'", *Zeitschrift für Sozialismus* 2 (22/23), pp. 725–733.

Orlova-Smirnova, Mariia (1986), "Pamiati Sergeia Aleksandrovicha Nilusa i Eleny Aleksandrovny Nilus. (Iz materialov Samizdata)", *Pravoslavnyi put' za 1985 god*, pp. 54–69.

Østbø, Jardar (2016), *The New Third Rome: Readings of a Russian Nationalist Myth*, Stuttgart: ibidem Verlag.

Panchenko, Aleksandr (2016), "The Computer Called The Beast: Eschatology and Conspiracy Theory in Modern Religious Cultures", *Forum for Anthropology and Culture*, 12, pp. 186–200.

Petrovsky-Shtern, Yohanan (2010), *Lenin's Jewish Question*, New Haven and London: Yale University Press.

Pierrard, Pierre (1970), *Juifs et catholiques français. De Drumont à Jules Isaac (1886–1945)*, Paris: Fayard.

Pipes, Daniel (1997), *Conspiracy: How the Paranoid Style Flourishes and Where It Comes From*, New York: Free Press.

Platonov, Oleg A. (1999), *Ternovyi venets Rossii. Zagadka Sionskikh protokolov*, Moscow: Rodnik.

——(2001), *Ternovyi venets Rossii: Istoriia tsareubiistva*, Moscow: Èntsiklopediia Russkoi Tsivilizatsii.

Platt, Kevin (2000), "Antichrist Enthroned: Demonic Visions of Russian Rulers", in: Pamela Davidson, ed., *Russian Literature and its Demons*, New York and Oxford: Berghahn Books, pp. 87–124.

Poliakov, Léon (1980), *La causalité diabolique. Essai sur l'origine des persécutions*, Paris: Calman-Lévy.

——(1985), *The History of Anti-Semitism, vol. 4: Suicidal Europe, 1870–1933*, Oxford: Oxford University Press.

Polovinkin, Sergei (1995), *Sergei Aleksandrovich Nilus (1862–1929). Zhizneopisanie*, Moscow: Izd. Spaso-Preobrazhenskogo Valaamskogo monastyria.

Raas, Emil and Georges Brunschvig (1938), *Vernichtung einer Fälschung. Der Prozess um die erfundenen "Weisen von Zion"*, Zurich: Die Gestaltung.

Radziwill, Catherine (1921), "Les Protocoles des Sages de Sion", *La Revue Mondiale*, 15 March, pp. 151–155.

Reitblat, Abram (1994), "Litvin, Savelii", in: *Russkie pisateli 1800–1917. Biograficheskii slovar'*, vol. 3 K-M, Moscow: Bol'shaia Rossiiskaia Èntsiklopediia, pp. 368–369.

Reventlow, Ernst zu (1923), "Um die Geheimnisse der Weisen von Zion", *Reichswart*, 4 (24), p. 3.

Reznik, Semyon (1996), *The Nazification of Russia: Antisemitism in the Post-Soviet Era*, Washington, DC: Challenge Publ.

Ribuffo, Leo P. (1979–80), "Henry Ford and 'The International Jew'", *American Jewish History* 69, pp. 437–477.

Richards, Guy (1972), *The Hunt for the Czar*, London: Sphere.

Rogge, Oetje John (1961), *The Official German Report*, New York and London: Thomas Yoseloff.

Rollin, Henry (1939), *L'Apocalypse de notre temps. Les dessous de la propagande allemande d'après des documents inédits*, Paris: Gallimard. New edns. Paris: Allia 1991 and 2005.

Rosenberg, Alfred (1923), *Die Protokolle der Weisen von Zion und die jüdische Weltpolitik*, Munich: Deutscher Volksverlag, Dr. E. Boepple.

Ross, Steven J. (2017), *Hitler in Los Angeles. How Jews Foiled Nazi Plots Against Hollywood and America*, New York and London: Bloomsbury.

Rossman, Vadim (2002), *Russian Intellectual Antisemitism in the Post-Communist Era*, Lincoln and London: University of Nebraska Press.

Ruotsila, Markku (2001), *British and American Anticommunism Before the Cold War*, London: Frank Cass.

——(2004), "Mrs Webster's Religion: Conspiracist Extremism on the Christian Far Right", *Patterns of Prejudice* 38 (2), pp. 109–126.

Russkaia doktrina (2016), *Russkaia doktrina. Gosudarstvennaia ideologiia èpokhi Putina*, Moscow: Institut russkoi tsivilisatsii.

Ruud, Charles (2009), *Fighting Words. Imperial Censorship and the Russian Press, 1804–1906*, Toronto: University of Toronto Press.

Ruud, Charles and Sergei A. Stepanov (1999), *Fontanka 16. The Tsar's Secret Police*, Montreal and Kingston: McGill-Queen's University Press.

Schmitt, Carl (2015), *Glossarium. Aufzeichnungen aus den Jahren 1947 bis 1958*, eds., Gerd Giesler and Martin Tielke, Berlin: Duncker & Humblot.

Schörle, Eckart (2009), "Internationale der Antisemiten. Ulrich Fleischhauer und der 'Welt-Dienst'", *WerkstattGeschichte* 51, pp. 57–72.

——(2010), "Erfurt – ein 'Mekka der Antiiudaisten'? Die antisemitische Propagandazentrale von Ulrich Fleischhauer", *Mitteilungen des Vereins für die Geschichte und Altertumskunde von Erfurt* 71 (18), pp. 108–136.

Sedgwick, Mark (2004), *Against the Modern World. Traditionalism and the Secret Intellectual History of the Twentieth Century*, Oxford: Oxford University Press.

Segel, Benjamin (1924), *Die Protokolle der Weisen von Zion kritisch beleuchtet. Eine Erledigung*, Berlin: Philo.

Seraphim (Eugene Rose) (1991), "Znaki iavleniia besov", *Nauka i religiia* 2, pp. 6–9.

——(1996), *Orthodoxy and the Religion of the Future*, 7th edn., Platina, CA: Saint Herman of Alaska Brotherhood.

——(2003), "Contemporary Signs of the End of the World", *The Orthodox Word* 228, pp. 12–45.

Shchedrin, Andrei (2002), "Dar profeta", in: *... I dany budut zhene dva kryla. Sbornik k 50-letiiu Sergeia Fomina*, Moscow: Palomnik, pp. 24–26.

Shnirel'man, Viktor (2017), *Koleno Danovo. Èskhatologiia i antisemitizm v sovremennoi Rossii*, Moscow: Izdatel'stvo BBI.

Shtyrkov, Sergei (2019), "Dukhovnoe videnie istorii kak diskursivnyi poriadok politicheskoi eskhatologii: ubiistvo sem'i Nikolaia II v pozdne- i postsovetskoi pravoslavnoi istoriografii", *Gosudarstvo, religiia, tserkov' v Rossii i za rubezhom* 37 (4), pp. 130–166.

Shumskii, Vladislav (1993), "Pechat' Antikhrista. Po povodu ubiistva v Optinoi Pustyni", *Den'* 22 (102), (6 –12 June), p. 5.

Siewert, Harald (1934), "Die Beichte eines kleinen Weisen von Zion", *Völkischer Beobachter* 357/358 (23/24 December), p. 1.

Singerman, Robert (1981–82), "The American Career of the 'Protocols of the Elders of Zion'", *American Jewish History* 71, pp. 48–78.

Skuratovskii, Vadim (2001), *Problema avtorstva "Protokolov sionskikh mudretsov"*, Kiev: Dukh i litera.

Slater, Wendy (2007), *The Many Deaths of Tsar Nicholas II. Relics, Remains and the Romanovs*, London and New York: Routledge.

Sliozberg, Genrich (1933), *Dela minuvshikh dnei. Zapiski russkogo evreia*, vol. 2, Paris: Petropolis.

Solov'ëv, Vladimir (1988), "Kratkaia povest' ob antikhriste", in: idem, *Sochineniia v dvukh tomakh*, vol. 2, Moscow: Mysl', pp. 736–759.

Stein, Alexander (1936), *Adolf Hitler: Schüler der "Weisen von Zion"*, Karlsbad: Graphia.

Sukhotin, Lev (1908), *Rod dvorian Sukhotinykh. (Ottisk iz Rodoslovnoi Knigi Tul'skogo Dvorianstva)*, Moscow: M.V. Baldin.

Szajkowski, Zosa (1974), *Jews, Wars and Communism. Vol. 2: The Impact of the 1919–20 Red Scare on American Jewish Life*, New York: Ktav.

Taguieff, Pierre-André (2004), *Les "Protocoles des Sages de Sion". Faux et usages d'un faux*, Nouvelle édn., Paris: Berg International-Fayard.

———(2020a), *Hitler, les Protocoles des Sages de Sion et Mein Kampf. Antisémitisme apocalyptique et conspirationnisme*, Paris: Puf.

———(2020b), *Criminaliser les Juifs. Le mythe du "meurtre rituel" et ses avatars (antijudaïsme, antisémitisme, antisionisme)*, Paris: Hermann.

———(2021), *Les théories du complot*, Paris: Que sais-je?

Tikhomirov, Lev (1999a [1911]), "K voprosu o masonakh", in: idem, *Khristianstvo i politika*, Moscow: Alir, pp. 328–331.

——— (1999b), "V poslednie dni (Ėskhatologicheskaia fantaziia)", in: idem, *Khristianstvo i politika*, Moscow: Alir-Oblizdat, pp. 393–538.

———(2004), *Religiozno-filosofskie osnovy istorii*, Moscow: Airis-press.

Tikhon (Georgii Shevkunov) (1993), "Nevidimaia bran'", *Literaturnaia Rossiia* 20, (21 May), pp. 6–7.

Thing, Morten (2014), *Antisemitismens bibel: Historien om smædeskriftet Zions Vises Protokoller*, København: Informations Forlag.

Ul'ianova, Liubov' (2021), "Arkhivnaia nakhodka: neizvestnyi variant 'Protokolov sionskikh mudretsov'", *Russkii sbornik. Issledovaniia po istorii Rossii* 30 (2021), pp. 553–558.

Velichko, Vasilii (1903), *Vladimir Solov'ëv: zhizn' i tvoreniia*, 2nd edn., Saint Petersburg: Tsinzerling.

Vinberg, Fedor (1922), *Krestnyi put'. Chast' pervaia: Korni zla*, Munich: Oldenbourg.

The Vision of our Holy Father John, Wonderworker of Kronstadt. http://www.orthodox.net/articles/vision-of-st-john-of-kronstadt.html, last accessed 21 September 2021.

Vries de Heekelingen, Herman de (1938), *Les Protocoles des Sages de Sion – constituent-ils un faux?*, Lausanne: A. Rochat-Pache.

Warburg, Gustav (1939), *Six Years of Hitler: The Jews Under the Nazi Regime*, London: George Allen & Unwin.

Webman, Esther, ed., (2011), *The Global Impact of The Protocols of the Elders of Zion: A century-old myth*, London and New York: Routledge.

Williams, Robert C. (1969), "Tödtli – A Berne Defender of the *Protocols*", *Wiener Library Bulletin* 23, pp. 67–71.

Wistrich, Robert S. (2008), "Dialogues in Hell: Zionism and Its Double", *Midstream*, May/June, pp. 9–13.

Yablokov, Ilya (2018), *Fortress Russia: Conspiracy Theories in Post-Soviet Russia*, Cambridge: Polity Press.

Zhevakhov, Nikolai (1936), *Sergei Aleksandrovich Nilus. Kratkii ocherk zhizni i deiatel'nosti*, Novyi Sad: S. Filonov.

Zipperstein, Steven J. (2018), *Pogrom. Kishinev and the Tilt of History*, New York and London: Liveright Publ. Co.

Zweig-Strauss, Hanna (2007), *Saly Mayer (1882–1950). Ein Retter jüdischen Lebens während des Holocaust*, Cologne: Böhlau.

Index

For Product Safety Concerns and Information please contact our EU
representative GPSR@taylorandfrancis.com
Taylor & Francis Verlag GmbH, Kaufingerstraße 24, 80331 München, Germany

9 7 8 1 0 3 2 0 6 1 1 6 0